AN ILLUSTRATED HISTORY OF

# SOUTHERN
## WAGONS
### Volume Two

**Frontispiece**  Thirty all-steel ballast hopper wagons were ordered from Hurst, Nelson & Company of Motherwell in 1903. This depicts the first example, No. 10510, as built. All were rebuilt in 1930 and most remained in service until around 1960, ten being transferred to the Isle of Wight after World War II.

*Hurst, Nelson & Co.*

# AN ILLUSTRATED HISTORY OF
# SOUTHERN
## WAGONS
## Volume Two: LBSCR and minor companies

Compiled by
G. Bixley  A. Blackburn  R. Chorley  M. King

# Oxford Publishing Co.

# AUTHORS' NOTES AND ACKNOWLEDGEMENTS

This, the second in our series of four volumes, describes those wagons taken over from the London, Brighton & South Coast Railway in 1923. It also describes wagons inherited from the various minor companies embraced at the Grouping; the three Isle of Wight concerns, the Plymouth, Devonport & South Western Junction Railway and the narrow gauge Lynton & Barnstaple Railway.

Whilst dealing with LBSCR wagons in the same format as used in **Volume One**, the minor companies have presented the authors with somewhat different problems of research. Official records were not always as thoroughly kept by the companies themselves, and recourse has been made to other sources of information, including rolling stock manufacturers, the Public Record Office and the University of Glasgow. The authors wish to place on record their thanks to the staff of both these establishments.

The Isle of Wight companies have posed one further problem. Although the number of wagons contributed to the Southern Railway was comparatively small, the complete lack of standardisation meant that few identical batches of wagons were owned; indeed we are left with the impression that, by 1923, there were no two vehicles exactly alike! Consequently, they cannot be detailed fully within the space at our disposal, so we have concentrated our efforts towards portraying a typical selection of vehicles, with the accent on those retained by the Southern Railway after the Grouping. In this we have been greatly assisted by Hubert Wheeller, who visited the Island in 1928 and recorded, with his camera, many of the goods vehicles shortly to be replaced by ex-LBSCR and LSWR types. Perhaps one day we might hope to see a book devoted exclusively to the rolling stock of the Isle of Wight, including the engines and carriages, for they were a fascinating collection of vehicles. The history of Isle of Wight goods wagons since 1923 is largely that of ex-LBSCR designs, therefore we have grouped both subjects into the same volume.

Finally, we would again like to thank all those individuals who have contributed to the production of these volumes. To the list of names credited in **Volume One** we wish to add three more; those of Jonathan Abson and R. C. Riley, both of whom have contributed their extensive knowledge of LBSCR stock, and Nigel Hearn for much valued assistance in sorting out the more obscure details of the Lynton & Barnstaple Railway vehicles.

*G. Bixley, A. Blackburn, R. Chorley, M. King*
*Woking*
*February 1985*

*Note.* All photographs from the Locomotive & General Railway Photograph collection are reproduced by courtesy of Messrs David and Charles Ltd.

Typesetting by:
Aquarius Typesetting Services, New Milton, Hants.

Printed in Great Britain by:
Biddles Ltd., Guildford, Surrey.

Published by:
Oxford Publishing Co.
Link House
West Street
POOLE, Dorset

# Contents

**Plate 1**  A general view of Brighton Carriage & Wagon Works yard, photographed in the early years of this century. Only one 'foreign' wagon is visible (a GWR two plank open), the remainder are of LBSCR origin. They include open 'A' Nos. 04051 and 5154, open 'D' No. 229 and 'D²' type opens Nos. 2994 and 3072. Note the LBSCR tarpaulins and the recently ciphered number on wagon No. 4051, indicating that it has been relegated to the duplicate list. It also carries a restricted use instruction: 'For use by Loco & Carriage Dept. only'.

*Lens of Sutton*

**Title Page**  Ex-LBSCR E1 class 0-6-0T No. W2 *Yarmouth* is seen at Newport (Isle of Wight) on 14th September 1937, heading a coal train from Medina Wharf. The open wagons are all of LBSCR origin.

*S. W. Baker*

**Plate 2** A rare example of an LBSCR mainland wagon which received a full repaint in early British Railway livery, photographed officially at Ashford Works in 1948. No. S22045 was built in 1921, part of a batch of 500 steel-underframed opens completed by the Metropolitan Carriage, Wagon & Finance Company. Originally built with round ends and Williams patent sheet rail, SR Diagram 1368 was at first allocated. These fittings were removed at a later date, SR Diagram 1365 being issued to cover the alterations.

*National Railway Museum/Crown Copyright*

**Plate 3** Class K Mogul, No. 341 heads a 'down' main line goods train south of Hassocks, probably just before the Grouping. The 17 engines of this class were regularly used on heavy goods services from World War I until their sudden demise in 1962. The use of a brake van at each end of the train was a common feature on the LBSCR at the time, and indeed this was about the only possible use for the light Stroudley vans where heavy goods services were contemplated. A single van at the rear would have been practically useless as a brake.

*Authors' Collection*

# Chapter 1
## General Introduction to LBSCR Wagons

The London, Brighton & South Coast Railway has long been a favourite with railway enthusiasts. It is remembered chiefly for its small, well proportioned and colourful locomotives and for the neat appearance of its rolling stock. The average fare-paying passenger, however, will probably recall the line more for its unpunctuality and for the often spartan comforts of those externally attractive carriages. Like the locomotives, carriage stock development failed to keep pace with changing needs and, by the Grouping, compared unfavourably with the best that could be had on the neighbouring LSWR and SECR. The same is true of the goods rolling stock; development by William Stroudley in the 1870s set the standard for most goods vehicles which were to remain almost unaltered to the end of the Company's existence. Thus a van of 1882 looked very similar to one built in 1922, the major difference being the provision of more modern brakes and running gear on the later example. Bodywork, in contrast, would have scarcely altered in those 40 years. At the Grouping, therefore, the goods fleet presented a very uniform if somewhat dated appearance. On the credit side, all the stock was maintained in first class mechanical order.

The Company was, in reality, an extended outer suburban railway, operating an intensive passenger service throughout the South London suburbs and into East Surrey and Sussex. Heavy goods traffic was primarily confined to the main lines; between London and Brighton, eastwards to the commercial port of Newhaven and the towns of Eastbourne and Hastings, westward to the naval base of Portsmouth. At both extremities it was in competition with other companies, but elsewhere held a virtual monopoly of traffic. The major London goods depots were situated at Battersea Wharf and Willow Walk, the latter served by a branch off the main line near New Cross (now New Cross Gate) and reached by running powers over the SECR's Bricklayers Arms branch. A large marshalling yard at Norwood Junction mainly served the needs of the immense suburban coal traffic.

Coal, in common with practically all other railways, was by far the largest single goods traffic, most of which was carried in private owner wagons. Many of these were registered by northern firms based well away from the LBSCR area. Most of this traffic reached the Company's metals over the West London Extension, Lillie Bridge Sidings being the usual transfer point; however, it was not unknown for GWR, MR and LNWR engines to work through to Norwood Yard and occasionally as far as Three Bridges. Interchange with the Great Northern was possible via the City Widened lines and with the Great Eastern via the East London line. The LBSCR possessed some mineral wagons of its own, mostly used for carrying coal landed at Deptford Wharf, Littlehampton or Shoreham harbours. The supply of locomotive coal was, in the main, contracted out to Messrs Stephenson, Clarke & Company, and this came by rail from South Wales, often via the LSWR through Fratton or Chichester.

**Plate 4** An 'up' train of mineral empties passes South Croydon behind C2 class 0-6-0 No. 536 around 1920. There does not appear to be a single LBSCR wagon in the train. Fifty five of these engines were constructed between 1893 and 1902, and they were much in evidence on goods work. Most were later rebuilt into Class C2X and survived until the 1960s.

*Lens of Sutton*

Away from the main lines the Company served a rural and mainly agricultural community, adequately provided for by a couple of daily pick-up goods services. There was a considerable trade in timber, indeed wagons for this traffic were second in terms of numbers after the open goods vehicles. Cattle and poultry were also important, the latter especially from around Heathfield and Uckfield. Some vehicles for both these duties were Westinghouse fitted for running in passenger trains. Fully fitted goods trains were unknown on the LBSCR, but there were a few mixed trains and these were by no means confined to the branch lines. A prestige traffic was the so-called 'Grande Vitesse' perishables service between Newhaven Harbour and Willow Walk. Photographic evidence **(see Plate 5)** indicates that this was once a goods-rated traffic but in later years was almost exclusively carried in passenger-rated vans.

**Plate 5** This 1882 official picture depicts 'Grande Vitesse' goods van No. 1507. Nothing is known about this vehicle, but it appears to be a lengthened version of the standard covered goods wagon, equipped with Westinghouse brakes and passenger rated running gear. The wagon plate tells us that it was of 10 tons capacity and the axleboxes are lettered 'LB&SC' with the date, 1878. Note also the heavy self-contained buffers, typical fittings of the Stroudley era. By 1923, the number 1507 had been reallocated to an ordinary covered goods wagon to SR Diagram 1433.

*British Rail*

Special goods vehicles were confined to a handful of well wagons, four gunpowder vans, two glass wagons and a few flats designated for aeroplane traffic. In 1923, the Engineer's Department still possessed about 150 small dumb-buffered ballast wagons, some with a capacity of as little as 4 tons. High capacity wagons were rare; indeed in 1923 only one vehicle exceeded 20 tons capacity, this being the unique rigid eight-wheeled boiler trolley built as long ago as 1889. Some bogie bolster/rail wagons built in 1903 had been rated at 25 or 30 tons, but all were downrated to 20 tons capacity during World War I. Another interesting (and unique) vehicle was the bogie refrigerator van of 1905. This ended its career stripped of bodywork, joining the small fleet of aeroplane trucks. After the mass reconstruction of six-wheeled coaches into bogie stock in the 1908-10 period, some thought was evidently given to the conversion of the many redundant underframes. During these years, a six-wheeled ballast wagon and a six-wheeled triple bolster wagon appeared, both types utilising former carriage stock underframes. Neither design was perpetuated, the Company preferring its tried and trusted smaller vehicles.

The earliest years of LBSCR rolling stock development are best ascribed to the mechanical dark ages under John Chester Craven's iron rule, but with the appointment in February 1870 of William Stroudley to the post of Locomotive, Carriage & Marine Superintendent, measured progress began to emerge. Stroudley was a brilliant engineer and a great advocate of standardisation, applying this as much to the goods stock as to locomotives and carriages. The earliest known official photographs of goods wagons date from 1882 and the emergence of a house style (to coin a modern phrase) was already evident from them — and this remained a consistent feature throughout the rest of the Company's independent life. Few wagons from this era survived to become Southern Railway stock, but many of their descendants from the 1890s did so. However, as already stated, these wagons were often little altered from their immediate predecessors.

William Stroudley's career came to an abrupt end in December 1889, when he died during a visit to Paris whilst on Company busi-

ness. He had previously discussed retirement and had suggested Robert Billinton as a suitable successor. At the time, Billinton held the post of chief draughtsman to the Midland Railway at Derby Works, a similar position to that which he had held at Brighton several years previously. R. J. Billinton made many improvements to the Company's carriage stock, such as adopting a higher roof profile, six-wheeled and later bogie vehicles, but made few changes to the goods wagons. It should be mentioned, however, that the higher roof profile was eventually applied to the covered goods, cattle wagons and brake vans. The somewhat antiquated Stroudley brake vans were still in production until 1890, and Billinton replaced these with his own design from 1894. Nevertheless, examples of Stroudley's brake vans remained in service until the 1920s, being amongst the oldest stock taken over by the Southern Railway. One innovation which belongs to R. J. Billinton's term of office was the introduction of steel underframes. Between 1896 and 1901, over 1,800 such wagons were put into traffic. Five basic designs were involved and most were built by contractors. Bodywork was, of course, to the usual LBSCR specification, therefore these wagons did not look appreciably different to timber-underframed types. These remained almost the only steel-underframed wagons owned, except for a few special vehicles and some of post-1920 construction, the latter incorporating certain modern features and RCH (Railway Clearing House) details. Perhaps, surprisingly, but in common with many other early steel-underframed wagons, these 1896-1901 vehicles did not survive as long as contemporary stock on timber underframes, and withdrawal had commenced before the Grouping. The Company was not equipped to build large numbers of steel wagon underframes and continued to employ timber right up to and just beyond the Grouping. Relatively few other wagons were ordered from rolling stock contractors, most of these being special all-steel vehicles. One exception to this came during 1908/9, coincident with the removal of rolling stock construction from Brighton to Lancing Works, when a batch of 100 timber-underframed open wagons was supplied by the Metropolitan Amalgamated Carriage & Wagon Company of Birmingham.

**Plate 6** Stroudley C1 class goods engine No. 427 awaits the road away from Preston Park with an 'up' goods, at some date prior to its withdrawal in March 1911. The obligatory Stroudley brake van may be seen behind the tender. This van, LBSCR No. 151, was allocated SR number 55681 at the Grouping, but was scrapped in 1924 before being renumbered.

*Lens of Sutton*

In common with most other railways, the LBSCR eventually found it necessary to separate the work of the locomotive department from that of carriage and wagon construction, and in 1898 appointed Albert Harry Panter as Carriage & Wagon Works Manager. This was not, however, a complete separation and it was not until 1911, at the end of Douglas Earle Marsh's locomotive superintendency, that Panter assumed the title of Carriage & Wagon Superintendent, with autonomous powers. A. H. Panter was the son of William Panter, who had been in charge of LSWR carriage and wagon affairs since 1885. Panter, the son, had served with his father at Nine Elms and Eastleigh Carriage Works and had also worked on the design and production of pressed steel underframes with the Leeds Forge Company before joining the LBSCR. Despite this, steel underframes never really caught on at Brighton Works, and LBSCR rolling stock construction owed little to the practices of Eastleigh. There was just one notable exception to this statement as Panter produced some goods brake vans during 1915/16 having outside timber framing very reminiscent of LSWR designs of some 30 years earlier. A. H. Panter remained in charge of the Company's Carriage & Wagon Department until he retired shortly after the Grouping. Much of the organisation of the new Carriage & Wagon Works at Lancing, which opened in 1909, may be attributed to him.

Prior to 1909, all rolling stock construction was based at Brighton Works, with some minor repairs being executed at New Cross. The facilities at Brighton were very cramped and regularly led to protracted overhaul times, both for locomotives and rolling stock. Over the years, several investigations were conducted in an attempt to ease the overcrowding and to improve efficiency. Eventually, in 1902, land was acquired to the west of Lancing Station for the construction of a new Carriage & Wagon Works. This was brought into production in April 1909, the completion of the first new wagon being a well photographed event **(see Plate 7)**. There were also plans to resite the Locomotive Works alongside, but the intervention of World War I halted this scheme.

The Southern Railway therefore took over a modern, well-designed series of workshops which catered for all forms of rolling stock construction and repair. After 1927, the Southern Railway decided to concentrate wagon repair work at Ashford, leaving Lancing to deal mainly with passenger vehicles. From time to time some goods vehicles, in particular brake vans and covered goods, were built or repaired there, whilst the Works continued to produce wagon underframes which were then sent to either Ashford or Eastleigh for body construction and finishing. The Works continued to function until 1965, when it was run down and closed. Today, the site is a trading estate devoid of rail access. One interesting feature of Lancing was the workmen's train. Dubbed the 'Lancing Belle', it remained steam-worked throughout its existence, running four times each day between the Works and Brighton Station.

**Plate 7** The first wagon completed at Lancing Works, on 13th April 1909. It is No. 715, an 8 ton open 'A' wagon. Later allocated SR number 19834 and Diagram 1366, it ran until July 1937. Notice that the tare (i.e. unladen) weight has yet to be painted on. The three worthy gentlemen in the picture are probably workshop foremen, the bowler being the customary headgear for such staff during this period.

*British Rail*

**Plate 8** This view shows the testing of a new type of automatic coupling at Lancing, possibly about 1919 or 1920. Open 'A' wagon No. 085 is numbered in the departmental service stock list and carried the stencil 'Carr. Dept' at the right-hand end. If dated correctly, this wagon was formerly No. 6177, built in 1899, and transferred to service stock in 1916. It later became SR No. 01036s. The LBSCR departmental wagon list began at 01 and numbered over 200 vehicles.

*Authors' Collection*

**Plate 9** A typical grease-filled axlebox, as fitted to Diagram 1369 open wagon No. 0922s, the subject of **Plate 30** on **page 19**. This was one of the final grease box-fitted wagons, being completed in 1905. The Mansell wheels should also be noted. Most Stroudley boxes were similar in appearance but were lettered 'LB&SC' with the date of manufacture on the cover below the Company initials.

*G. Y. Hemingway*

**Plate 10** A No. 7 oil-lubricated axlebox, as used from 1905 onwards. This was by far the most common oil axlebox and was fitted to almost all vehicles of 8 and 10 tons capacity. The journal size was 8in. x 4in. Wagons of 12 and 15 tons were provided with the very similar No. 8 box, having 9in. x 4½in. journals.

*E. R. Lacey*

The somewhat retarded development of LBSCR wagons resulted in their playing little part in subsequent Southern Railway practice, and it was hardly surprising that ex-SECR and LSWR policies prevailed. The lack of RCH fittings and other features which were regarded as non-standard by the SR were to cause many maintenance problems, especially if a wagon required attention far from its home area. In the days before the adoption of common-user policies this seldom posed a problem, but by the 1920s an ex-LBSCR wagon could find itself in the north of Scotland for a considerable period of time. If, at such a location, the vehicle required major repairs involving, for example, replacement wheel sets, it was clearly a costly and time wasting procedure to send these north from Lancing. The Southern Railway decided to overcome these problems in two ways; either by utilising as many wagons as possible in departmental service, or by transferring the wagons to the Isle of Wight. Both courses of action would ensure that the annual mileage of any given vehicle was small, and would also allow them to remain within a limited geographical area. Economics, of course, dictated that it was impossible to utilise all LBSCR wagons in this manner, but nevertheless some 600 went to the Isle of Wight from 1924 onwards, and a considerably larger number entered departmental use during Southern Railway ownership. Those on the Island outlived their mainland counterparts by many years, examples of most designs remaining in service until the end of steam operation in 1966. — Few other LBSCR wagons remained in ordinary traffic for long under British Railways ownership, and it is worth recording that the official series of wagon photographs taken at Ashford Works during 1948/9 included very few ex-LBSCR designs.

The following table gives a breakdown of the number of LBSCR wagons taken into Southern Railway capital stock at the Grouping, and will be worthy of careful study by modellers wishing to portray a typical LBSCR goods yard scene. These figures are based on the SR renumbering registers and the totals shown on the diagrams, and should not be relied upon to the last digit. Figures quoted by the Company were not unknown to vary slightly depending on their source.

## TABLE ONE
### LBSCR Wagons taken into SR Stock after 1st January 1923 (including outstanding orders)

| | Capacity in Tons | | | | | | | | | | | |
| Vehicle Type | 4 | 6 | 7 | 8 | 9 | 10 | 12 | 15 | 20 | 30 | Totals | % of Total |
|---|---|---|---|---|---|---|---|---|---|---|---|---|
| Open Goods | - | 9* | - | 2,500 | - | 5,455 | - | - | - | - | 7,964 | 74 |
| Mineral | - | - | - | - | - | - | 225 | - | - | - | 225 | 2 |
| Covered Goods | - | - | 1 | 527 | - | 35 | - | - | - | - | 563 | } |
| Egg Vans | - | - | - | 20 | - | - | - | - | - | - | 20 | } 5½ |
| Insulated Vans | - | - | - | - | 2 | - | - | - | - | - | 2 | |
| Cattle Wagons | - | 400 | - | - | - | 20 | - | - | - | - | 420 | } 4¼ |
| Special Cattle Vans | - | - | - | 23 | 6 | - | - | - | - | - | 29 | } |
| Goods Brake Vans | - | - | 139* | - | 28 | 96 | 14 | 15 | 65 | - | 357 | 3¼ |
| Timber/Bolster Wagons | - | 377 | - | 131 | - | 126 | - | - | - | - | 634 | 6 |
| Road Vehicle Trucks | - | - | - | - | - | 123 | - | - | - | - | 123 | 1 |
| Plate Glass Wagons | - | 2 | - | - | - | - | - | - | - | - | 2 | } |
| Aeroplane Trucks | 3* | - | - | - | - | - | - | 1 | 3 | - | 7 | } ¼ |
| Machine/Well Wagons | - | - | - | - | - | - | - | - | 6 | 1 | 7 | } |
| Gunpowder Vans | - | - | 4 | - | - | - | - | - | - | - | 4 | } |
| ED Ballast Wagons | 75 | 71 | - | - | - | - | - | 112 | 30 | - | 288 | } |
| ED Ballast Brake Vans | - | - | - | 11 | - | - | - | - | 6 | - | 17 | } 3¾ |
| ED Rail/Sleeper Wagons | - | - | - | - | - | 15 | 75 | - | 12 | - | 102 | } |
| Totals | 78 | 859 | 144 | 3,212 | 36 | 5,870 | 315 | 127 | 122 | 1 | 10,764 | 100 |

Notes:

1. Figures marked * include some duplicate stock. At least 30 more open goods wagons were subsequently added to the SR renumbering list, some of which took numbers previously allocated to vehicles shown in the above totals.

2. These totals do not agree with the 1923 Company returns, partially because ED stock (non-revenue earning) was omitted from such returns.

3. Some wagons were withdrawn before receiving their allocated SR numbers, in particular those dating from Stroudley's term of office.

4. Some reclassification of stock occurred in the 1923-5 period. The 4 ton aeroplane trucks were formerly ED stock, whilst 6 rail wagons were transferred to departmental service. See relevant text for full details.

5. The 29 special cattle vans were reclassified as passenger stock shortly before the Grouping and remained so under SR ownership.

6. The Southern Railway ordered 600 open goods wagons to Diagram 1369 after the Grouping, details being as follows:
    250 x 10 ton open goods wagons ('partial renewals'). SR order No. L8.
    350 x 10 ton open goods wagons ('partial renewals'). SR order No. L27.
    Most were sent to the Isle of Wight within a year of completion.

# Chapter 2
## Livery, Running & Diagram Numbers

### LBSCR Wagon Liveries

Since the days of William Stroudley, LBSCR goods wagon liveries may be divided into three periods. The first covers the years before circa 1895, the second from at least 1897 to 1911, and the third from 1911 until the Grouping. In every case, the basic body colour was a shade of grey, but there were three very different lettering styles.

### The Stroudley era, and up to circa 1895

To this period belongs the very pale 'lavender grey' body colour, with black ironwork and running gear, together with the so-called 'illiterate' symbol. In Victorian times, several railways employed distinctive markings, as opposed to company initials, to identify their own goods stock and alone, of the Southern companies, the LBSCR favoured this practice. The symbol itself consisted of a white shield upon which was superimposed a red cross, the whole being placed within a blue circle, usually about 9in. in diameter. A smaller version appeared on vehicles with narrow side rails and also on the dumb-buffered ballast wagons. It was usually positioned to the left and high up on each side. The wagon number was normally placed below this in approximately 3in. white figures, shaded black. Apart from the wagon plate, centrally mounted on the solebar, the only other lettering carried was usually the tare weight, in plain white 3in. figures, towards the left-hand end of each solebar. A few vehicles, brake vans in particular, also carried the Company initials in the same style as the wagon number. The word 'Guard' was also carried as appropriate, with a slightly enlarged 'G'. The ends of goods brake vans were bright red, described by a contemporary observer as vermilion, and a similar colour was applied overall to Engineer's Department ballast wagons and brake vans. The latter carried the word 'Ballast' in 6in. letters; as usual white shaded black. It is not clear, however, if the ED bright red was the same shade as used on the ends of brake vans.

Few other brandings appeared on the wagons. The word 'machinery' was noted on many of the road vehicle/machinery trucks, and these sometimes also carried the Company initials as well as the illiterate symbol. Van roofs were white when ex-works, including stove chimneys, vents and lamp tops. The interiors of open wagons were left unpainted except for the black ironwork. Wagon plates were cast, oval in shape, and were attractively finished in bright blue, the raised lettering and surround being picked out in white. Some cattle wagons had rectangular plates, a style adopted universally from 1911 onwards. Many brake vans did not carry these plates, at least not

visibly. The vehicles in **Plates 5, 11, 17, 60, 66, 95 & 104** illustrate this style of livery. However, attention is drawn to the van in **Plate 5**, which has a very dark overall finish, possibly the contemporary carriage stock colour of mahogany, with plain white lettering.

### The period from circa 1895 to 1911

The basic body colour was changed to a darker shade of grey, officially termed lead colour. The exact date of this change is not known to the authors, but it seems to have been definitely associated with R. J. Billinton. His appointment as Locomotive, Carriage & Wagon Superintendent dates from 1890, so this would be the earliest possibility. The livery style was definitely being used by 1897. Ironwork was black, and this included the underframes of those wagons so constructed in the 1896-1901 period. Roofs, lettering and numerals were white. All revenue-earning wagons now carried the Company initials, usually in 9in. or 10in. high letters. From at least 1899 until 1902, these took the form LB&SCR**y**, but from 1903 this was abbreviated to LB&SCR. In some cases these letters were shaded black, several steel underframed covered goods and some brake vans being specifically noted. This also seems to have been a short-lived feature. The wagon number was normally 6in. high but was 9in. on brake vans. The latter style appears in **Plate 12**. Tare weights were 3¼in. high and rather strangely appeared on both the side sheeting and on the solebar. Brake vans had the word 'Guard' painted on each side door, shaded black in some cases. The ends were painted 'orange-red', possibly the same colour previously described as vermilion. The painting of brake van ends in a conspicuous colour ceased around 1904. Interiors of these vans were painted in a stone colour.

There were few other wagon brandings. The open wagon class letter (A, B, C, D, D²) was carried over the number in earlier years, but this practice appears to have ceased by 1908, although of course some wagons could still be seen carrying the letters for several years after that. The road vehicle/machinery trucks continued to be lettered 'Machinery', and the ballast brake vans were branded 'Ballast' in 8in. letters. Many ballast wagons did not carry the Company initials but were lettered ND or SD, denoting whether they were allocated to the Northern or Southern engineering districts. The 20 ton ballast hoppers and the 30 ton bogie rail wagons, built in 1903 by Hurst, Nelson, carried 6in. Company initials as well as the inscription 'Engineer's Dept.'; this, the number and tare were 3in. high.

**Plate 11** Stroudley covered goods wagon No. 1577, as running in July 1882. This carries the then standard light grey livery with the illiterate symbol but without Company initials. The tare weight does not show up in the picture but appears at the left-hand end of the solebar. This van was withdrawn in 1907, being replaced by a new vehicle bearing the same number. The later No. 1577 became SR No. 46255, and survived until 1941.

*British Rail*

Number plates continued to be painted blue until at least 1905, but were usually black from 1906 onwards. The last overhaul date was entered on the curb rail in italic script, prefixed 'B' for Brighton. It is very likely that N+ for New Cross was also used but 'L' for Lancing does not appear to have been applied, and wagons continued to carry the 'B' prefix.

**Plate 12**  Billinton 10 ton brake van No. 29, in 1903-11 livery. This was built in 1897 and remained in traffic until April 1937, being allocated SR Diagram 1568 and running number 55754. The overhaul date appears to be B 4/3/05. Note that the brake van on the right does not carry the word 'Guard' on the side door, possibly indicating that this photograph may date from post-1911.
*W. O. Steel Collection*

## The period from 1911 onwards

In 1911, it was reported in the railway press that the letters LBSC had been introduced by the Company. A specification issued in August of that year called for these letters to be painted 10½in. high on the 225 12 ton coal wagons built by Hurst, Nelson. These were to have had their numbers and tares painted 5½in. high, but there is some doubt whether this style was widely used **(see Plate 68)**. The standard form of the livery used 18in. letters, the number was normally 5in. high, and the tare weight 3½in. Some wagons, of course, did not have room for this arrangement. Machinery trucks, for example, had the Company initials and number 6in. high, whilst the capital letter of 'Machinery' was 3¾in. high, and the remainder of the word was 3in. high. Timber wagons (single bolsters) had 4½in. numbers and initials, and the tare was in 3in. figures. The absolute minimum was reached on the 1921 rail wagons which had 2¾in. initials and 1¾in. numbers and tare.

On goods brake vans the word 'Guard' was no longer carried, but the practice of painting the number in large figures continued. All new number plates were rectangular in shape. The seemingly pointless duplication of tare weights also ceased. The grey base colour was again darkened, possibly over a period of time, until by the Grouping it was a very dark colour indeed. One contemporary observer has recorded that it had a bluish tinge. The ironwork on the body sides was no longer blacked up, and this feature was often absent in earlier years.

There were very few exceptions to these standard liveries. Cattle wagons did not receive lettering on their ends until SR days, whilst the few insulated/refrigerator vans do not appear to have been given any special treatment. The bogie vehicle carried the words 'Perishable Traffic' on the body side and it is probable that the four wheelers were similarly lettered. The authors have no information on the gunpowder vans. Shortly before the Grouping, the special cattle vans were reclassified as passenger stock and should have received umber livery. It is probable that they were always finished in passenger stock livery as they were built for service in passenger trains.

A full study of Southern Railway liveries must wait until **Volume Four,** but a brief outline appeared in **Volume One.** It is worth noting that the Southern Railway reversed the LBSCR wagon plates and painted the new number on the reverse, together with the letter 'B' below it, denoting Brighton Works, and that the wagon was of LBSCR origin. For some reason, by the mid-1930s many LBSCR wagons had lost their plates, so these details were painted directly on to the solebars — a practice employed from 1923 on those goods brake vans without plates.

### Wagon Tarpaulins

Little has been recorded about these, but they were probably black and carried large white Company initials and numbers. A considerable total was in service, due mainly to the large number of sheet rail-equipped open wagons and the small total of covered goods wagons. These tarpaulins featured a large coloured (white?) cross, to assist in centering the sheet. An example is shown in **Figure 1,** along with other examples of LBSCR wagon lettering.

**Figure 1** Some examples of LBSCR wagon lettering.

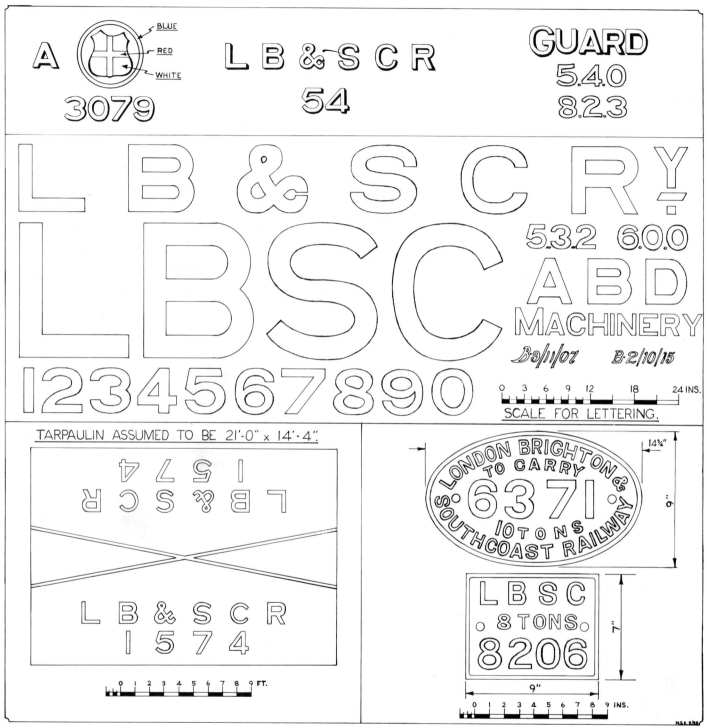

## Numbering — LBSCR and SR

LBSCR wagon numbering followed the most common pre-Grouping system — the next new wagon taking the next vacant number, regardless of type. No attempt was made to sort each class of vehicle into separate batches of numbers. As wagons were scrapped so their numbers were reallocated to new vehicles, again not necessarily of the same type. Many consecutive batches of numbers would be allocated to new stock built on the capital account, but in time some of these would be scrapped and replaced by others charged to the renewal account, taking the same number as the original vehicle. These replacements were seldom of the same type; often open goods wagons would be replaced by vans as dictated by changing traffic requirements. At the Grouping, most numbers above 8500 were still in consecutive batches, having been built on the capital account in the 1896-1923 period and, for the most part, had not been replaced by newer vehicles. The highest number allocated was 11114, completed in 1921. Below No. 8500 it was a very different story; there were very few consecutively numbered batches of identical wagons remaining in traffic. Goods and ballast brake vans were the exceptions to the general rule, as these had their own series of numbers, reaching a maximum of 393 at the Grouping. True to form, however, these numbers were also very mixed and even the most recent in construction took numbers widely scattered in the list. Other Engineer's Department ballast, rail and sleeper wagons were numbered in the general sequence, and did not employ a separate series of numbers.

Some wagons, usually those approaching the end of their working lives, were relegated to a duplicate list, their numbers being ciphered (a '0' added in front of the existing number). This allowed the original number to be reused for a new vehicle. Another ciphered list was also used for departmental stock, commencing at 01 and comprising over 200 vehicles. These were mainly yard wagons at Brighton or Lancing Works, dock wagons at Newhaven, beach wagons at Eastbourne (Crumbles Sidings, from whence the LBSCR obtained shingle for ballasting purposes), loco ash wagons, stores vans and the like. In many cases, these vehicles carried brandings indicating that they were to be used only for that particular purpose. A typical example may be seen in **Plate 8.**

The Southern Railway renumbered the entire stock after the Grouping, sorting the wagons by origin, type and in ascending order of capacity in the form shown in **Table Two.** Not surprisingly this procedure took several years to complete, and wagons in pre-Grouping livery were not uncommon until the early 1930s. Some LBSCR wagons have been noted carrying their old numbers but otherwise in full SR livery during the 1923-7 period, the number being prefixed 'B' to distinguish them from ex-LSWR and SECR wagons which might possibly carry the same pre-Grouping number. The initial SR renumbering scheme was very logical, but soon became obscured by changes, additions and the reuse of numbers for new stock. Fuller details of SR numbering may be found in **Appendix 1** on **pages 104-106,** along with the diagram numbers, which were arranged along similar lines. Examples of LBSCR numbering will be given in the relevant chapters.

## Diagrams — LBSCR and SR

From time to time the LBSCR issued a large drawing entitled 'Diagrams of Wagon Stock', upon which were drawn small-scale diagrams of the various types of goods wagon, together with leading dimensions, carrying capacities and the totals of vehicles in service. These details were periodically updated; new stock being added and withdrawn types being deleted as necessary. Each diagram was merely a representative sketch of the wagon concerned and, before World War I at least, were not even given individual diagram numbers. As such, their use for modelling and identification purposes is rather limited. By 1917, however, diagram numbers were being used and these will be found in the text, cross-referenced to the subsequent Southern Railway diagram numbers. The latter will be used for identification purposes throughout this series of volumes. As was the usual practice with diagrams, many detail differences were ignored, and it was by no means unknown to find, for example, wagons with different wheelbases or body construction included together on the same LBSCR diagram. As far as the Southern companies were concerned, the LBSCR was probably the worst offender in this field.

The Southern Railway took these diagrams one step further, in general separating the various different types and producing new diagrams to cover the variants. However, by no means all changes in construction were faithfully recorded on the new diagrams. The Southern Railway diagram numbering system is summarised in **Table Two,** being arranged in exactly the same way as the running numbers. In time, SR-built and converted stock was incorporated into the list, so by the time of nationalisation quite a few running numbers and a handful of diagram numbers had been allocated twice.

## TABLE TWO
### Summary of Southern Railway Diagram and Wagon Running Numbers

| Type of Vehicle | SR Diagram Numbers | Diagram Numbers of Ex-LBSCR Stock | SR Running Numbers | Running Numbers of Ex-LBSCR Stock |
|---|---|---|---|---|
| Open goods and mineral wagons | 1301-1400 | 1362-1375 | 1-42000 | 18729-19078 and 19273-27711 |
| Covered goods wagons | 1401-1460 | 1433-1436, 1457 | 42001-50000 | 46191-46773 |
| Refrigerator, banana and insulated vans | 1461-1480 | 1471 | 50001-51000 | 50594-50595 |
| Ventilated meat vans | 1481-1500 | None | 51001-51500 | None |
| Cattle wagons | 1501-1540 | 1527-1528 | 51501-54500 | 52882-53301 |
| Goods brake vans | 1541-1590 | 1564-1577 | 54501-57000 | 55586-55942 |
| Bolster, timber and batten wagons | 1591-1640 | 1616-1621 | 57001-60000 | 58277-58910 |
| Road vehicle trucks | 1641-1670 | 1661 | 60001-61000 | 60423-60545 |
| Special vehicles (glass, aero, well, machinery) | 1671-1700 | 1684-1689 | 61001-61200 | 61066-61085 |
| Gunpowder vans | 1701-1710 | 1705 | 61201-61300 | 61261-61264 |
| Miscellaneous wagons | 1711-1730 | None | 61301-61500 | None originally, 61361 later |
| Ballast wagons, ballast brakes and plough vans | 1731-1780 | 1751-1760 | 61501-63500 | 62532-62856 |
| Locomotive coal wagons | In open goods range | In open goods range | 63501-64500 | None originally, some from 1925 |
| Rail and sleeper wagons | 1781-1849 | 1798-1803 | 64501-64800 | 64642-64737 |
| Service and departmental stock (mostly SR conversions) | 1850-2000 | Few diagrams allocated | 1s-1999s 01s-01290s | Various |

*Notes:*

1. Duplicate stock not generally included, a few were later added to the list. Some of these reused numbers in the blocks given above.
2. Vehicles built to LBSCR designs between 1923 and 1926 are included.
3. Fifty open goods wagons were converted to carry propeller cases between 1941 and 1945, being renumbered as SR Nos. 5071-5120 in the former LSWR open wagon series.
4. SR diagram numbers from 1-1300 and from 2001 onwards were allocated to passenger stock.

# Chapter 3
## Open Goods and Mineral Wagons

Open goods wagons, together with a few hundred mineral wagons, formed over 75 per cent of LBSCR goods rolling stock at the Grouping, a very high proportion of the total, and far in excess of the LSWR percentage. The SECR also had a similarly high figure but, in their case, the total included some 2,000 mineral wagons. The distinction between open goods and mineral wagons appears to have changed somewhat at the Grouping; the LBSCR considering its 'C' class open as a coal wagon (i.e. mineral) — the SR describe these as open goods wagons. The only other LBSCR mineral wagon design was a standard RCH seven plank vehicle. For the purpose of description we have considered both as mineral wagons, but the table of statistics reproduced on **page 5** groups them with the open wagons, following Southern Railway practice. Details of both types will be found at the end of this chapter.

This leaves us with nearly 8,000 open goods wagons in capital stock, plus several hundred in departmental service. They are remarkable if only for their similarity, all being 15ft. 5in. long over headstocks and, apart from two small groups of three and four plank

vehicles, all the rest had five side planks. The majority also had round ends and a tarpaulin sheet rail — fittings that were removed from 1926 onwards as wagons passed through shops. This officially resulted in a new diagram number being allocated, but in practice this was not always recorded, the SR register entry being confined to the words 'with square ends', no new diagram number being stated. The new diagrams were, however, issued to the traffic department. The process of removing the round ends took many years and many vehicles were scrapped in the 1940s still carrying them. It was by no means uncommon to find wagons in service without sheet rails but retaining the round ends.

The LBSCR identified the various types of open and mineral wagons by a classification letter, which also appeared over the number on the vehicle itself. After about 1908, this system of identification began to fall out of use, and by 1911 it was unusual to see a wagon carrying its classification letter. Details of the classes are as below.

| Class | Type of Vehicle | Capacity (Tons) | LBSCR Diagram Numbers (see note) |
|---|---|---|---|
| A | Five plank open goods with round ends and sheet rail | 8 and 10 | 1,2,29 and one other |
| B | Three plank dropside open goods | 6 | 5 |
| C | Six plank coal wagon (mineral) | 10 | 6 |
| D | Four plank open goods with round ends | 6 | 4 |
| D²* | Five plank open goods with square ends | 8 | 3 |
| E* | Seven plank mineral wagon (to RCH specification) | 12 | 7 |

Note:    All references to LBSCR diagram numbers pertain to those in use from circa 1917 onwards.
Earlier diagrams do not appear to have been individually numbered.

*These two codes are shown on some copies of LBSCR diagrams only, and do not seem to have been
widely used or painted on the vehicles concerned. It is very unlikely that the
'E' class letter was ever used as these wagons date from 1911/12.

The Southern Railway found that the 'A' class comprised at least four slightly different designs plus a modern 1920/1-built version, and allocated five separate diagrams to cover these. The removal of round ends, plus a couple of conversions and downratings brought the total of SR diagrams to sixteen instead of nine in pre-Grouping days. Two of these diagram numbers (1365 and 1374) were in fact issued twice. No 'B' class open wagons became SR capital stock at the Grouping, although a couple were subsequently so allocated; no SR diagram number was issued for them.

For the purpose of study we intend to divide these vehicles into four groups, as follows:

1. Three plank dropside open goods wagons
2. Four plank round-ended open goods wagons
3. Five plank round and square-ended open goods wagons
4. Six and seven plank mineral wagons

### Three plank dropside open goods wagons

These were the 'B' class open goods wagons and they only just managed to become SR stock at the Grouping. Eight vehicles appear in the Southern Railway service stock register as numbers 01088s-01095s. At least two and possibly one more were transferred to capital stock in 1925. However the records are not clear and the wagons may never have received their allocated numbers. All were considered as duplicate stock by the LBSCR, having had their existing numbers ciphered between 1920 and 1922. As such, they were described as 'beach wagons' and may have been employed on the Crumbles Siding at Eastbourne, from whence the LBSCR obtained shingle for track ballasting. They may also have been barred from travelling on the main line.

**Plate 13** 'B' class open wagons are rather elusive, but one is visible in this view of Portsmouth Town goods yard, taken in the first decade of this century. It is loaded with a furniture container belonging to Pratt Brothers who describe themselves as removal contractors. The joint nature of this station is well illustrated by the presence of both LBSCR and LSWR stock, with a G6 class 0-6-0T locomotive shunting.
*Lens of Sutton*

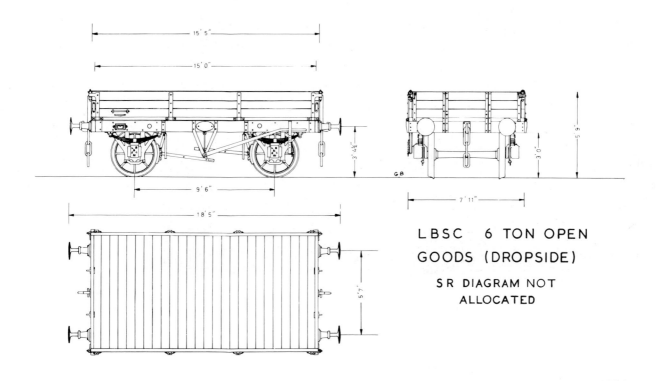

LBSC  6 TON OPEN
GOODS (DROPSIDE)
SR DIAGRAM NOT
ALLOCATED

**Figure 2**  A drawing of the 'B' class open goods wagon.

These dropside wagons were among the first steel-underframed wagons owned by the LBSCR, thirty being added to stock in the half-year ending December 1896. Most LBSCR stock was ordered on a half-yearly basis, therefore an entry of 'into stock 12/96' could indicate any time between July and the end of December, or even very early in 1897. The SR register records the wagons as being built at Brighton; if so then these are almost the only steel-underframed wagons built by the Company. LBSCR numbers were 8301-30 and all had a capacity of 6 tons. Like many other early steel-underframed vehicles, they appear to have suffered badly from the effects of corrosion, and were being scrapped as little as 20 years later. Many contemporary timber-underframed wagons lasted for 30-40 years. LBSCR numbers 8301-30 were reallocated to new five plank open wagons in 1922, indicating that all the 'B' class vehicles had been scrapped or relegated to the duplicate list by then.

**Examples of numbering (for full details of SR numbering of LBSCR wagons see Appendix 1)**

| SR Service Stock Number, 1923 | LBSCR Number | Date Built | Brake Gear | SR Capital Stock No. | Date Transferred | Withdrawn | Remarks |
|---|---|---|---|---|---|---|---|
| 01088s | 08321 | 1897 | DB | 19275 | 1925 | - | Ex-8321 in 1922 |
| 01090s | 08311 | 1896 | DB | - | - | 1924 | Ex-8311 in 1920 |
| 01093s | 08324 | 1897 | DB | 19277 | 1925 | - | Ex-8324 in 1920 |
| 01094s | 08318 | 1896 | DB | 19278 | 1925 | - | Ex-8318 in 1921 |

**Explanation of brake gear codes (these will be used throughout this volume)**

SB = Single block and lever one side
DB = Double block and lever one side
 F = Freighter — Double block and lever both sides
 M = Morton clutch brake
SC = Screw brake (mostly on brake vans and bogie vehicles)

SL = Any type of brake with a lever on one side
ES = Any type of brake with a lever on both sides
 W = Westinghouse braked
WP = Westinghouse piped

**Four plank round-ended open goods wagons**

The LBSCR 'D' class open wagons were a very common type in former years. Like the 'B' class, only a handful survived in 1923 and all these are noted in LBSCR registers as duplicate stock. Construction of this design ceased in 1897, after which type 'D²' was built instead. Just nine wagons were allocated Southern Railway running numbers at the Grouping but there was a fairly sizeable total in departmental use, and a few of these were transferred back into capital stock during 1924/5. Perhaps even more remarkable is that the last survivor was not deleted from stock until 1935, having outlasted all other vehicles of its class by some seven years! SR Diagram 1365 was allocated, however the authors have never seen a copy of it and it is possible that the drawing was not issued. Two versions of the LBSCR diagram existed, one showing an overall width of 7ft. 3in. and a later one giving this dimension as 7ft. 9in.

**Plate 14** This interesting period pi[cture] shows open 'D' wagon, No. 459, be[ing] loaded with hay at Arundel, probably [in] the summer of 1903. The overhaul d[ate] on the wagon appears to be 20/5/[03] but it may be 1905 as the last digi[t is] obscured. Note the Mansell whe[els,] timber brake block and curved 'W' iro[n.] No. 459 was built in the six months e[nd]ing June 1893 and was scrapped in 1[9..] after a relatively short working life of [...] years.

*Authors' Collect[ion]*

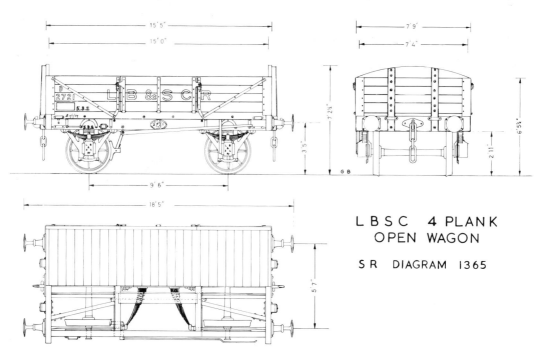

LBSC 4 PLANK
OPEN WAGON

SR DIAGRAM 1365

**Figure 3**

**Plate 15** Another 'D' class open wagon, photographed at Selsey in February 1935, in the livery of Colonel Stephen's Hundred of Manhood and Selsey Tramway, also known by the less prosaic title of the West Sussex Railway. Almost certainly the vehicle was sold prior to 1923, and is thought to pre-date No. 459. Self-contained buffers are fitted. The body strapping and axleboxes are also different from wagon No. 459.

*Lens of Sutton*

**Plate 16** A superb official broadside view of wagon No. D2721, photographed in 1907 and carrying a typical livery of the 1903-11 period. Points of note are the overhaul date of 11/1/07, ironwork not picked out in black, and the cast-iron brake block. Notice also that this wagon has diagonal strapping, unlike the two 'D' class opens so far illustrated. Possibly No. 2721 is 7ft. 9in. wide, the other (and earlier) vehicles being 7ft. 3in. wide. It was built in 1897 and ran until 1917.

*British Rail*

### Examples of numbering (for full details of SR numbering refer to Appendix 1)

| SR Number | LBSCR Number | Date Built | Brake Gear | Withdrawn | Remarks | SR Number | LBSCR Number | Date Built | Brake Gear | Withdrawn | Remarks |
|---|---|---|---|---|---|---|---|---|---|---|---|
| 19273 | 1310 | 1888 | SB | 7/23 | Duplicate | 19281 | 3527 | 1892 | SB | 3/35 | |
| 19279 | 3049 | 1897 | Poss. DB | 3/27 | | 0903s* | 03* | 1895 | SB | 7/28 | ED Stock |

*Departmental stock numbers. Original LBSCR number was 4370.

Further examples of LBSCR numbering are 1,229, 1052, 1602-9, 2850, 2902, 2921-5, 3211, 3306, 4019, 4379, 5791.
All these were replaced by new stock before the Grouping.

#### Five plank round and square-ended open goods wagons

These were by far the largest group, and may be considered par excellence the most characteristic LBSCR goods wagon. All exhibit the same family likeness which has its origins in the early years of William Stroudley's superintendency. The last new design appeared in 1920, but in general features if not in detail, it was recognisably from the same stable.

**Plate 17** The earliest known official photographs of LBSCR rolling stock date from 1882. Included in this series was open 'A' wagon No. 6627, a very early example of a five plank, 10 ton round-ended open wagon. The pale grey livery with the 'illiterate' symbol and black ironwork show up clearly. Indeed this colour scheme could not have been bettered for its photogenic qualities. Note the fact that, apart from the plate, no Company identification letters are carried. The loose chain sheet rail is also noteworthy. This wagon was scrapped some time before the Grouping, and it may well have been withdrawn and replaced by a new vehicle bearing the same running number before 1900.

*British Rail*

The following table lists the various Southern Railway diagrams issued to cover these five plank open wagons, arranged in approximate chronological order. It also includes the rebuilds and conversions which appeared subsequent to the Grouping.

| SR Diagram | LBSCR Diagram | Capacity (Tons) | Wheel base | Type of Underframe | Type of End | Known Construction Period | Remarks |
|---|---|---|---|---|---|---|---|
| 1367 | 3 | 8 | 9ft. 6in. | Timber | Square | 1896-1905 | Original square-ended design. LBSCR Class 'D²'. |
| 1371 | 2 | 10 | 9ft. 6in. | Steel | Round | 1896-1900 | Built by contractors. Some later to D1375. |
| 1375 | | 8 | 9ft. 6in. | Steel | Round | Downrated 1924-30 | Ex-Diagram 1371. |
| 1370 | 1 | 10 | 9ft. 6in. | Timber | Round | 1898-1904 | Some later to D1363. |
| 1363 | | 10 | 9ft. 6in. | Timber | Square | Converted from 1926 | Ex-Diagram 1370. |
| 1366 | 29 | 8 | 9ft. 3in. | Timber | Round | 1905-1912 | Some later to D1364. |
| 1369 | 1 | 10 | 9ft. 3in. | Timber | Round* | 1905-1926 | Some later to D1362/4/74. Some built by SR. |
| 1364 | - | 8 and 10 | 9ft. 3in. | Timber | Square | Converted from 1926 | Ex-Diagrams 1366/9. |
| 1374 + | - | 10 | 9ft. 3in. | Timber | Square | Rebuilt in 1934 | Seven plank coal wagon, ex-Diagram 1369 for IOW. |
| 1362 | - | 10 | 9ft. 3in. | Timber | Round | Converted 5-7/41 Reverted 1/45-5/46 | Ex-Diagram 1369, for carrying propeller cases |
| 1368 | Not known | 10 | 9ft. 0in. | Steel | Round | 1920-1921 | Built by contractor. Some later to D1365. |
| 1365 + | - | 10 | 9ft. 0in. | Steel | Square | Converted from 1926 | Ex-Diagram 1368. |

\* Many SR-built wagons did not have round ends but were allocated to Diagram 1369  
\+ Second allocation of diagram numbers

Note: In later years it was not uncommon to find square-ended wagons officially allocated to Diagrams 1366/8/9/70.

The propeller case conversion to Diagram 1362 merely involved cutting two holes in the floor planking, to enable one blade of each propeller to pass through. The propellers themselves were loaded in cradles specially made for the purpose. The conversions were carried out under SR order No. E1489 and all were renumbered into a series from 5071-5120. After the war, they were no longer needed and reverted to their former numbers when returned to Diagram 1369. Regrettably the authors have been unable to trace any photographs of the conversions.

Plate 18 Square-ended open wagons were not very numerous in pre-Grouping days, comprising about 15 per cent of the total open goods stock. A total of 1,100 was extant in 1923, being allocated SR Diagram 1367. They were, in effect, an 8 ton version of Diagram 1370 minus the round ends and sheet rail. LBSCR No. 5551 was built in 1902 and became SR No. 21766, lasting until April 1927. The large Company lettering dates this picture as post-1911. Double block brake gear is provided.

*H. V. Tumilty Collection*

Plate 19 Diagram 1367 open wagon No. 0581s, photographed about 1945 as part of Fratton ARP train. Many LBSCR open wagons entered SR departmental service stock from the 1930s onwards, and this vehicle may be regarded as typical. Built in 1900 as LBSCR No. 5191, it later became SR No. 21675 and was transferred to departmental use in July 1937. Its original cost is recorded as £83. Note that the wagon retains grease axleboxes; oil lubricated ones were not fitted until 1905.

*Lens of Sutton*

**Plate 20** Between 1896 and 1900 a total of 1,250 steel-underframed open 'A' wagons was constructed by the Birmingham Railway Carriage & Wagon Co. and Messrs Cravens of Sheffield. They were very distinctive, having inside diagonal strapping and a heavy steel backstay across each end, clearly visible in this view which illustrates LBSCR departmental No. 015 at New Cross Gate in 1925. Formerly No. 8767, it entered Loco. Dept. use in 1923, and later carried SR number 0915s.

*L. E. Brailsford*

**Figure 4**

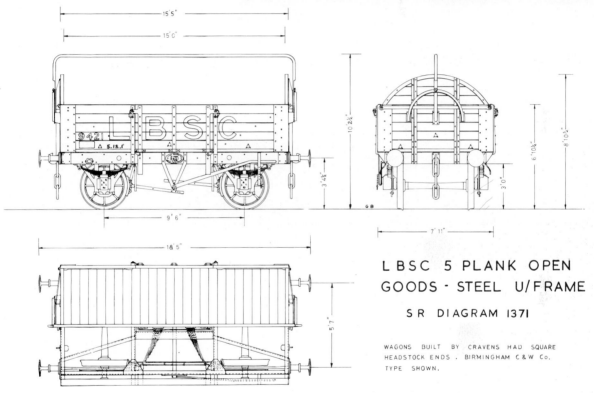

LBSC 5 PLANK OPEN
GOODS - STEEL U/FRAME

SR DIAGRAM 1371

WAGONS BUILT BY CRAVENS HAD SQUARE
HEADSTOCK ENDS . BIRMINGHAM C&W Co.
TYPE SHOWN.

All these wagons were allocated capital stock numbers when new, as follows:

| | |
|---|---|
| LBSCR Nos. 8501-8800 | Built by Cravens, 1896 |
| LBSCR Nos. 8801-8900, 9051-9550 | Built by BRCW, 1897 |
| LBSCR Nos. 10000-10349 | Built by BRCW, 1900 |

A total of 900 remained in capital stock at the Grouping, being allocated SR Diagram 1371. Many of the remainder had already entered LBSCR service stock and some of these were reinstated in SR capital stock during the period 1923-26, taking numbers already vacated by withdrawn wagons.

**Plate 21** This illustrates a typical vehicle to Diagram 1375, having been downrated to 8 tons capacity. Built by Cravens in 1896, and allocated LBSCR number 8797, it was first allocated SR number 26341 but was downrated to 8 tons in 1929, and instead received SR number 64482 in the loco. coal wagon series. It is pictured in this condition, with a hybrid LBSCR/SR livery. Note the 'To work between Portslade & Lancing only' instruction. In September 1932, it was renumbered yet again as 641s in the service stock list, finally being scrapped at the end of 1935. The last example in capital stock did not survive much longer, being condemned in 1938.

*Lens of Sutton*

**Plate 22** Timber-underframed open 'A' wagons with a wheelbase of 9ft. 6in. were built from 1898 until 1904. Southern Railway Diagram 1370 was allocated. Withdrawal of these began before 1923 but over 1,000 became SR property. No. 5751 was built in 1902, later becoming SR No. 24190, and was scrapped in 1931. This official photograph, taken in 1907, shows the single vee hanger used by the LBSCR for many years. A large boss ensured that the push rod remained horizontal, this being visible in the centre of the vee hanger. A few wagons to this design were equipped with patent either-side brake gears. Details may be found on **page 31.** The pale-coloured rectangle below the number was a 'chalking board' for recording instructions and destinations.

*British Rail*

**Plate 23** An open wagon to SR Diagram 1370 in pre-war Southern livery, No. 25202 was photographed in the works yard of Chas. Roberts & Company, Wakefield. Formerly LBSCR No. 6883 it dates from 1901. As built, it had double block brake gear but this was altered to the Freighter type in August 1933. The axlebox journals were also changed from 8in. x 3½in. to 8in. x 4in. at some time. This probably indicates the replacement of grease axleboxes (illustrated) by oil-lubricated ones. It ran until September 1945, a late survivor to this diagram.

*Authors' Collection*

**Plate 24** A similar open wagon in departmental use at Lancing Works, still carrying LBSCR lettering in October 1935. Numbered 01047s in the SR service stock list, it was built in 1899 as LBSCR No. 6328, and entered departmental stock in 1916, being renumbered 096. Single block brake gear is provided. Withdrawal came in December 1935.

*H. C. Casserley*

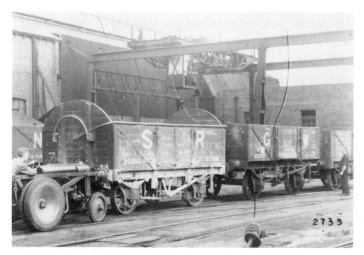

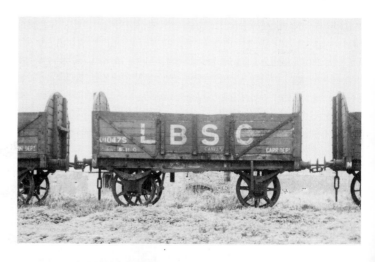

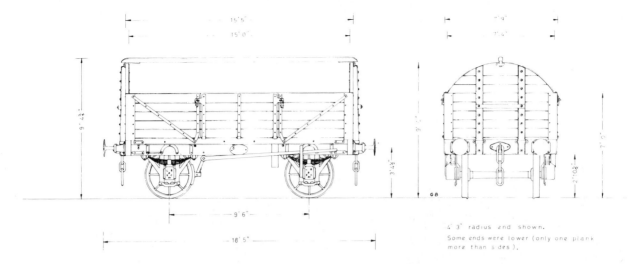

LBSC 5 PLANK OPEN WITH BAR    SR DIAGRAM 1370

**Figure 5**    A drawing of SR Diagram 1370 showing the timber sheet rail fitted to early examples. Later wagons had Williams' patent sheet rails. On removal of the round ends, SR Diagram 1363 was allocated.

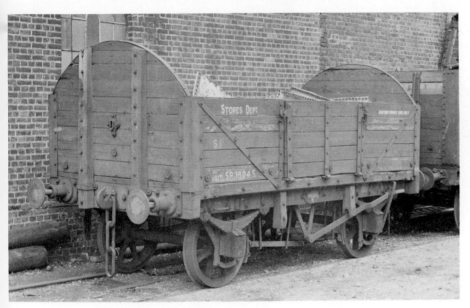

**Plate 25** SR departmental stores wagon No. 1804s at Ashford Works in 1948. This has lost its sheet rail but retains round ends; a not uncommon arrangement. Built in 1903 as LBSCR No. 1363, it was first allocated SR number 24750 as an open goods wagon, but was subsequently transferred to a loco. coal wagon, instead numbered 64245. In March 1943, it was further transferred to departmental stock and given the number 1804s. In this guise, it survived in occasional use at Ashford until February 1952.

*J. H. Aston*

In 1905 the wheelbase of open goods wagons was altered from 9ft. 6in. to 9ft. 3in., probably to give adequate clearance for the buffer springs which were moved from between the middle cross-members to a position immediately behind the headstocks. This wheelbase remained standard for all subsequent timber-underframed open 'A' wagons. Both 8 and 10 ton versions were produced, Diagrams 1366 and 1369 respectively being allocated.

**Plate 26** An 8 ton wagon, No. 1881, photographed with the letters SR but otherwise retaining an LBSCR lettering layout. The overhaul date of N + 16/1/23 is visible below the tare weight. It is the earliest known photograph of a wagon carrying the letters 'SR', and may still be finished in LBSCR grey livery. The wagon number may be prefixed 'B' on the plank above, as this has been noted on other LBSCR stock in the 1923-7 period. The subsequent SR number was 20364, and it ran from 1906 until 1945. Note the oil axleboxes, double block brake gear and the SECR tarpaulin sheet. Freighter brakes were added in July 1930 and the wagon was uprated to 10 tons in March 1937.

*Authors' Collection*

**Plate 27** A close-up view of the end detail of open wagon No. 19353 to Diagram 1366, photographed at New Cross Gate in 1936. Note the small pulley-shaped rope hooks used to secure the tarpaulin sheet. Built in 1908 as LBSCR No. 89, this vehicle survived until December 1947. In common with most Diagram 1366 open wagons, it was uprated to 10 tons capacity in the late 1930s. Cost when new is recorded as £53.

*E. R. Lacey*

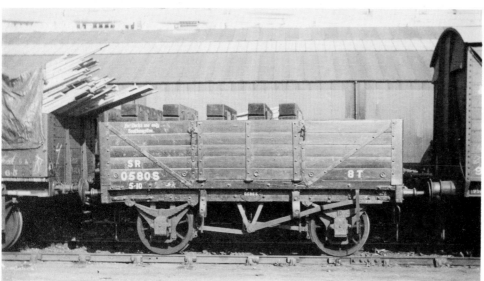

**Plate 28** A 1907-vintage open wagon, No. 0580s, in departmental service at Southampton Docks, shortly after transfer to service use in June 1937. The former SR traffic department number was 20154. This wagon has lost its round ends and sheet rail, and was reallocated to SR Diagram 1364. It remained at Southampton until withdrawal in April 1946.

*E. R. Lacey*

**Plate 29 (Below)**   The last 8 ton open wagons were completed in 1912, and were among the first LBSCR open wagons to be fitted with outside knees; a development that was applied to most subsequent batches of 10 ton wagons. This Ashford 1948 picture shows No. S19475 in SR brown livery, but with the Company initials replaced by the 'S' prefix to the number. Built in 1912 as LBSCR No. 235, it was uprated to 10 tons and modified to Diagram 1364 in the 1930s. Freighter brakes were provided when built, but three wagons to Diagram 1366 had patent either-side gear fitted. Details of these wagons may be found on **page 31**.

*National Railway Museum/Crown Copyright*

**Plate 30** The 10 ton version to SR Diagram 1369 was destined to become the most numerous LBSCR wagon, finally comprising over 3,500 examples. Construction ceased in 1926. SR No. 0922s was built in 1905 as LBSCR No. 6902. It has grease axleboxes and, unusually, Mansell wheels. Allocated SR traffic department number 25220, it was reallocated to the locomotive department in August 1928. When photographed in 1935 at Stewarts Lane, it had Freighter brakes but was built with brake gear on one side only. It has also been down-rated to 8 tons.

*G. Y. Hemingway*

**Plate 31** In 1908/9 the Metropolitan Amalgamated Railway Carriage and Wagon Company built 100 open wagons to SR Diagram 1369. Their numbers were 10770-10869, later SR Nos. 25834-25933. Wagon No. 10773 was delivered in April 1908 and ran until February 1937. It is of interest to note that these wagons were built with Freighter brakes, yet Lancing continued to build opens with brake gear on one side only until as late as 1911, the last year that this practice was allowed. LBSCR Nos. 10555-10766 (SR Nos. 25622-25833) were typical of LBSCR construction during this period. Other points to note are the oil axleboxes, black painted ironwork, and the lack of the 'A' classification letter.

*Authors' Collection*

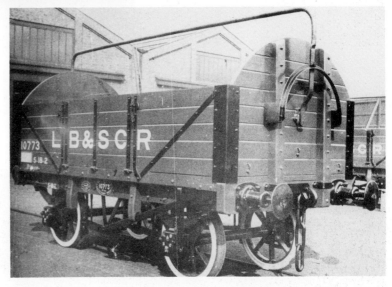

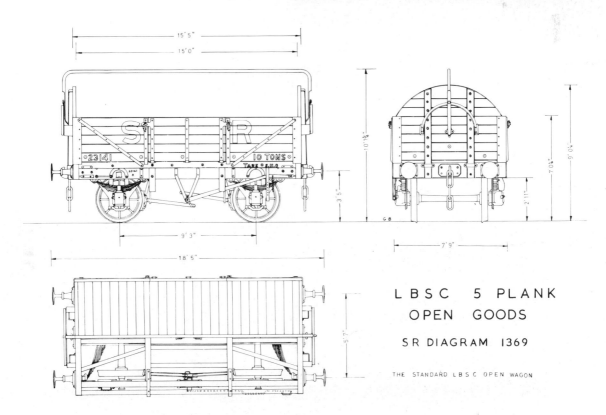

LBSC 5 PLANK
OPEN GOODS

SR DIAGRAM 1369

THE STANDARD LBSC OPEN WAGON

**Figure 6** A typical open wagon to Diagram 1369, showing the strapping detail used from 1912 onwards.

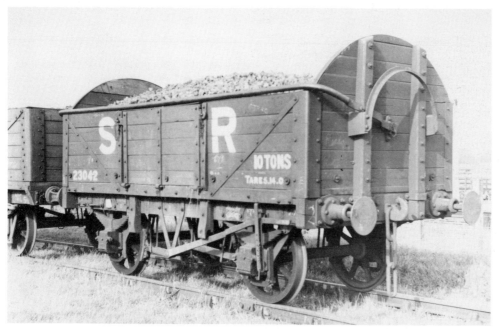

**Plate 32** Diagram 1369, open wagon No. 23042, at Cardington (Bedford) in 1938, carrying SR pre-1936 lettering, but grey instead of the usual brown livery. Several wagons have been so recorded, and this matter is discussed further on **page 20** of **Volume One.** The former number of this vehicle was 4148, and it dates from 1915. In its final years, it was boarded for carrying 'Tarred stone only', being withdrawn in May 1948. Many elderly open wagons were so branded as this material contaminated the timbers and rendered the wagons useless for other traffic. Note the double 'vee' hangers, a development dating from around 1914. However, there were earlier examples.

*A. E. West*

**Plate 33** Wagon No. 24290, a 1914-built example with single 'vee' hangers. The LBSCR number was 5881. This vehicle was one of the 50 converted to carry propeller cases during World War II. From July 1941 until January 1945, it carried the number 5120, after which it reverted to the number 24290. Withdrawal came in August 1948.

*W. O. Steel Collection*

**Plate 34** Relatively few LBSCR open wagons received post-1936 lettering as applied to No. 23062, seen at Cardington in 1938. This was formerly LBSCR No. 4172 of 1921 vintage. This also has double 'vee' hangers but the inside ones were bolted to the back of the solebar instead of on the middle longitudinals as on wagon No. 23042. All three open wagons illustrated on this page have external side knees. Earlier wagons had inside knees like most contemporary coal wagons **(compare with Plates 30 & 31).** This change dates from around 1912.

*A. E. West*

**Plate 35** General withdrawal of open wagons to Diagrams 1364/6/9 took place during the years 1944-7, and relatively few survived to receive British Railways livery on the mainland. One that did so was No. S23682 (ex-LBSCR No. 5078 of 1921; cost new £256). It is probably typical of the last survivors, having lost its sheet rail and round ends. Most, if not all of the SR-built wagons of 1924-6 omitted these features when new. The 4-hole disc wheels date from the 1920s, and were relatively uncommon on Diagram 1364/9 wagons.

*National Railway Museum/Crown Copyright*

**Plate 36** This illustrates three open wagons to Diagram 1369 at Newport (IOW), and their almost perfect paint finish was typical of the Isle of Wight before World War II. Note the different positions of the letters 'SR'. Wagon No. 28422 shows Lancing practice whilst No. 27819 follows the usual Ashford layout. A total of 450 of these vehicles was shipped to the Island between 1924 and 1931, a re-build to Diagram 1374 was sent in 1934 **(see below),** a further single example was sent in 1937, and a final six followed in 1947.

*Authors' Collection*

All Isle of Wight wagons, except the first 20 sent over, had square ends; these 20 were later altered to match. These, plus the next 56 examples were brand-new, but the remainder had all worked on the mainland for varying periods. SR Nos. 26119-23/31-45 had round ends, Nos. 18980-19017/33/34/60-75 came next and kept their mainland numbers, but almost all the rest were renumbered on transfer. The exceptions were the solitary vehicles sent over in 1934 and 1937.

**Plate 37** Few major reconstructions of LBSCR wagons took place. Just two vehicles were rebuilt as seven plank coal wagons to Diagram 1374. One went to the Isle of Wight (No. 27545), and the other (No. 18780) remained on the mainland.

*A. B. Macleod*

21

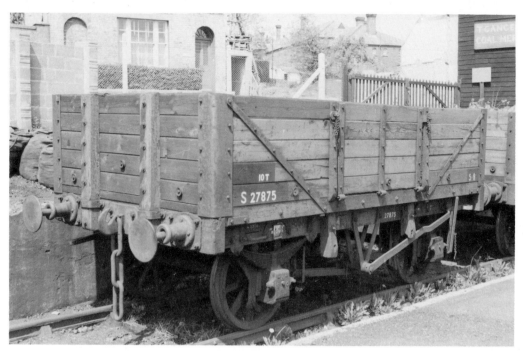

**Plate 38** Isle of Wight transfer No. S27875 one of the last wagons shipped over in 1931 is pictured in 1955. It is in BR grey livery with black patches, upon which the lettering is superimposed. These wagons were used mainly to carry coal on the Island, and it was normal procedure for them to stand loaded at Medina Wharf for long periods. This practice resulted in considerable damage to the wagons and undoubtedly contributed to the poor post-war condition of many of them. By 1955, only 320 remained in service, and this was reduced to 150 by 1962.

*R. E. Lacy*

**Plate 39** A dozen Isle Of Wight Railway open wagons were retained for loco. coal traffic until the late 1950s. Upon their withdrawal, some LBSCR open wagons were renumbered to replace them, taking those same numbers. No. S64398 assumed this number in 1959 and was photographed at Medina Wharf in August 1966, just four months before the demise of steam working. The letters MP denote 'Motive Power' and that the wagon was restricted to carrying locomotive coal only. Its rather worn black livery contrasts with the light grey of No. S28446 in the background. The previous number carried by the loco. coal wagon is not recorded in the Southern Railway registers.

*T. Gough*

The last development in LBSCR open wagons came during 1920/1 when 500 steel-underframed vehicles were ordered from the Metropolitan Carriage, Wagon & Finance Company, as they were then known. Although obviously to LBSCR specification, they were much more modern in design than any other LBSCR open wagons. Amongst other features they had RCH journal spacing (6ft. 6in. — most other LBSCR wagons employed 6ft. 3in.) and volute buffer springs. All had either-side brake gear and 4-hole disc wheels. SR Diagram 1368 was allocated.

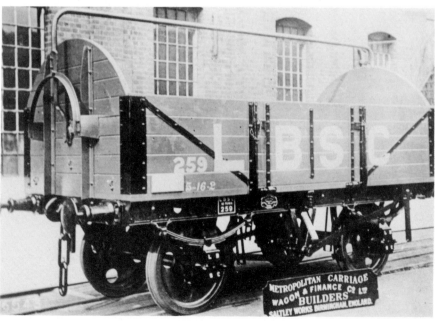

**Plate 40** This shows LBSCR No. 259 when new. Note the paint finish with a return to black ironwork. The later SR number was 21823 and the wagon ran until January 1950.

*W. O. Steel Collection*

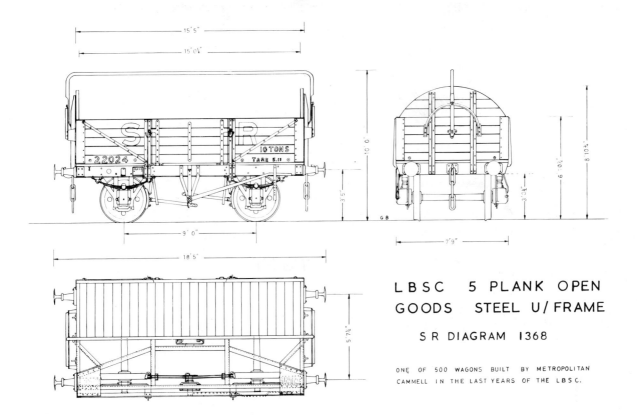

LBSC 5 PLANK OPEN
GOODS STEEL U/FRAME

S R DIAGRAM 1368

ONE OF 500 WAGONS BUILT BY METROPOLITAN
CAMMELL IN THE LAST YEARS OF THE LBSC.

**Figure 7**   The steel-underframed open wagon design of 1920.

**Plate 41**   An open wagon to Diagram 1368 in pre-1936 SR livery at Cardington (Bedford) in 1939. SR No. 21962 was originally LBSCR No. 1175, and ran until August 1947. Being of more modern design, most of these wagons were still in service in the late 1940s. A small number had their round ends removed and were reallocated to SR Diagram 1365 **(see Plate 2)**. Odd examples of these were still in use in the late 1950s.

*A. E. West*

**Plate 42**   This picture, taken at Wimbledon in June 1946, illustrates a very rare occurrence; that of a wagon identifiably carrying an incorrect number. Diagram 1368 was allocated SR numbers 21792-22291, so No. 22653 is most definitely out of sequence. The SR register indicates that No. 22653 is a timber-underframed wagon to Diagram 1369! Just what the correct number should be, and how the error came to be made, the authors cannot say. There is clearly a prototype for everything! The lettering is also unusual, being a wartime 3in. 'economy' style.

*D. Cullum*

## Examples of numbering (for full SR numbering details refer to Appendix 1)

| SR Diagram | SR Number | LBSCR Number | Date Built | With-drawn | Brake Gear | Notes |
|---|---|---|---|---|---|---|
| 1362 | 5075 | 3367 | 6/17 | 12/45 | F | Ex-SR No. 22582, 1941. To loco. coal No. 64203, 3/45 |
| 1362 | 5101 | 3934 | 12/12 | 10/48 | F | Ex-SR No. 22884, 1941. Reverted to No. 22884, 5/46 |
| 1363* | 24155 | 5712 | 1902 | 10/37 | DB, F 9/31 | To departmental wagon No. 1171s |
| 1363* | 24450 | 6049 | 1902 | 6/43 | DB, F 5/30 | 'Tarred stone only. Return empty to SR' |
| 1364* | 19802 | 678 | 6/08 | 9/37 | DB, later F | Ex D1366. To departmental wagon No. 0798s |
| 1364* | 25729 | 10662 | 6/07 | 4/37 | DB, F -/28 | 'Tarred stone only. Return empty to SR' |
| 1365* | 22045 | 1734 | 12/20 | 5/48 | F | To departmental wagon No. 846s (**see Plate 2**) |
| 1366 | 19574 | 359 | 6/09 | 1/49 | DB, F -/28 | |
| 1366 | 19834 | 715 | 4/09 | 7/37 | DB | To departmental wagon No. 0585s (**see Plate 7**) |
| 1367 | 20927 | 1760 | 1899 | 7/23 | DB | SR number not carried |
| 1367 | 21291 | 2906 | 1902 | 3/50 | DB, F 3/31 | One of the last survivors |
| 1367 | 21748 | 5497 | 1898 | 2/38 | DB, F 8/35 | To departmental wagon No. 1226s |
| 1368 | 21792 | 1 | 12/20 | 3/45 | F | 'To work between Dartford & Totton only' 5/42 |
| 1368 | 21988 | 1382 | 12/20 | 2/51 | F | Sheet rail retained |
| 1369 | 22638 | 3449 | 12/20 | 2/50 | F | Sheet rail retained |
| 1369 | 23124 | 4236 | 6/21 | c1963 | F | Waterloo & City line match truck from 1/59 |
| 1369 | 23221 | 4338 | 6/21 | 6/46 | F | Original cost, £275 |
| 1369 | 23575 | 4933 | 6/21 | 8/46 | F | Cement traffic Millbrook to Hoo (Johnson Sidings) from 10/32 |
| 1369 | 23905 | 5394 | 6/14 | 3/47 | F | |
| 1369 | 24032 | 5579 | 6/05 | 12/46 | DB, F 9/31 | Built with grease axleboxes, later oil |
| 1370 | 23716 | 5133 | 1901 | 3/43 | DB, F 8/30 | To departmental wagon No. 1815s |
| 1370 | 23776 | 5224 | 1898 | 6/38 | DB, F 1/31 | To loco. coal wagon No. 64318, 9/33 |
| 1370 | 23859 | 5338 | 1898 | 9/32 | DB | To loco. coal wagon No. 64472, 12/26 |
| 1370 | 24010 | 5556 | 1901 | 1/42 | DB, F 8/31 | To departmental wagon No. 1710s |
| 1370 | 24495 | 6097 | 1902 | 3/38 | DB, F 10/31 | To departmental wagon No. 1240s |
| 1371 | 26213 | 8558 | 1896 | 3/35 | DB | |
| 1371 | 26294 | 8720 | 1896 | 9/32 | DB | To loco. coal wagon No. 64479, 5/29 |
| 1371 | 26951 | 10184 | 1900 | 3/34 | DB | To departmental wagon No. 774s |
| 1374 | 18780 | - | 1925 | 1948 | F | Rebuilt from Diagram 1369, 1934 |
| 1375 | 26250 | 08622 | 1896 | 3/31 | DB | To loco. coal wagon No. 64477, 5/29 |

\* Dates of removal of round ends not recorded in SR register
Many wagons to Diagrams 1371/5 were recorded as duplicate stock, having ciphered LBSCR numbers
For numbering of Isle of Wight transfers see **Appendix 1**

## Six and seven plank mineral wagons

Only 425 mineral wagons were owned by the Company during the period from 1898 until the Grouping, although the 'D' class open wagons were, at some time, referred to by the title 'Coal D', indicating that they were used for mineral traffic. As previously mentioned, the Southern Railway only considered the seven plank open as a mineral wagon, reclassifying the six plank vehicle as an open goods wagon. Details of both types are as follows:

| SR Diagram | LBSCR Diagram | Capacity (Tons) | Built by | Date | LBSCR Numbers | SR Numbers | Remarks |
|---|---|---|---|---|---|---|---|
| 1372 | 6 | 10 | Ashbury Carriage & Iron Company | 1898 | 8340-8390 | 27086-27236 | Steel underframes |
| 1374 | - | 8 | | | 9851-9999 | In D1372 range | Ex-Diagram 1372 |
| 1373 | 7 | 12 | Hurst, Nelson & Co. | 1911/12 | 10870-11094 | 27237-27461 | RCH design. |

A total of 151 six plank 'C' class coal wagons remained in service at the Grouping.

**Figure 8** is a drawing of the six plank wagon. In common with other early steel-underframed wagons they suffered an early demise, the last example being withdrawn from capital stock in 1935. Some were downrated to 8 tons from 1925 onwards, and others became loco. coal wagons, renumbered in the 64XXX series. A few entered departmental stock and survived somewhat longer than the rest.

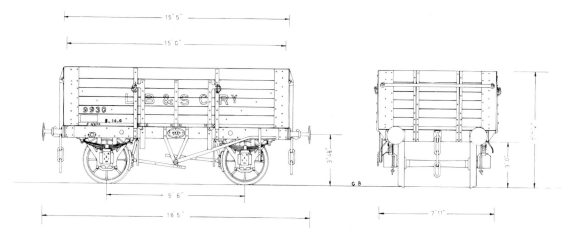

## LBSC 6 PLANK OPEN GOODS
### SR DIAGRAM 1372

A total of 225 mineral wagons to RCH specification was ordered from Messrs Hurst, Nelson & Company of Motherwell in 1911. Rather interestingly they were constructed to SECR Company drawings, probably because at the time this contractor was building a large number of similar wagons for that railway. It was therefore expedient to increase the order and charge the additional wagons to the LBSCR account. All became SR stock and a few lasted until 1948.

**Plate 43** This is a maker's photograph of SECR No. 13578. This later became SR No. 16897 to Diagram 1357. No photographs of the LBSCR vehicles are known to the authors, and it must be presumed that they were identical. **Figure 9** depicts these vehicles and is based on the SECR general arrangement drawing with LBSCR amendments overprinted. When new, all wagons were labelled 'Empty to Deptford'.

*Hurst, Nelson & Co.*

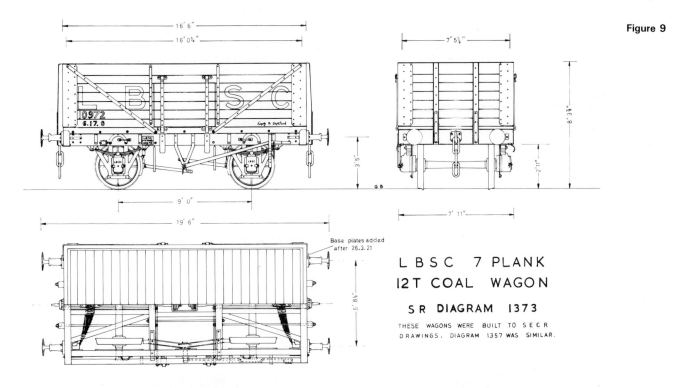

**Figure 9**

L B S C  7  P L A N K
12 T  COAL  WAGON

SR  DIAGRAM  1373

THESE WAGONS WERE BUILT TO SECR DRAWINGS. DIAGRAM 1357 WAS SIMILAR.

### Examples of numbering (for full SR numbering details refer to Appendix 1)

| SR Dia. | SR No. | LBSCR No. | Date Built | Withdrawn | Brake Gear | Notes | SR Dia. | SR No. | LBSCR No. | Date Built | Withdrawn | Brake Gear | Notes |
|---|---|---|---|---|---|---|---|---|---|---|---|---|---|
| 1372 | 27089 | 8344 | 1898 | 3/35 | DB | 3 | 1373 | 27247 | 10880 | 6/12 | 2/30 | F | |
| 1372 | 27141 | 9869 | 1898 | 1/28 | DB | | 1373 | 27248 | 10881 | 6/12 | 5/46 | F | |
| 1374 | 27086 | 08340 | 1898 | 6/31 | DB | 1 | 1373 | 27430 | 11063 | 6/12 | 1/48 | F | |
| 1374 | 27179 | 9918 | 1898 | 11/29 | DB | 2 | 1373 | 27440 | 11073 | 6/12 | 9/48 | F | 3 |

*Notes:* 1. Renumbered as loco. coal wagon No. 64475, 5/27.
2. Renumbered as loco. coal wagon No. 64493, 5/29.
3. Probably the last survivor to the diagram.

Many wagons to Diagrams 1372/4 were recorded as duplicate stock, having ciphered LBSCR numbers.

# Chapter 4
## Covered Goods Wagons

LBSCR covered goods wagons were possibly even more standardised than the open wagons, almost every vehicle being 18ft. 4in. long over headstocks and having a wheelbase of 9ft. 9in. They formed a very small group of vehicles compared to most other railways, a mere 5½ per cent of the total goods fleet; less than 600 wagons in all. This small percentage may be partially explained by the fact that so many open wagons carried sheet rails and could therefore provide covered accommodation (of a sort), if necessary. However, it is equally possible that the volume of perishable goods traffic did not warrant large numbers of covered goods vehicles. Certainly, ventilated and insulated, as well as continuously-braked goods vans were a rare sight on the Brighton line. Such perishables traffic that existed travelled primarily in passenger-rated rolling stock.

Six Southern Railway diagrams concern us in this section, one of which was an Isle of Wight conversion from a cattle wagon. There was also one conversion from a goods brake van, which may have received a Southern Railway diagram number. Details are as follows:

| SR Diagram | LBSCR Diagram | Capacity (Tons) | Designated Traffic | Known Construction Period | Brake Gear | Remarks |
|---|---|---|---|---|---|---|
| + | - | 7 | Covered Goods | Rebuilt 6/23 | H | Ex-D1564 Brake van |
| 1433 | 8 | 8 | Covered Goods* | 1878-1915 | H or W | Several variations |
| 1434 | 9 | 8 | Covered Goods | 1900-1901 | H | Steel underframes |
| 1435 | 10 | 8 | Egg Traffic | 1898-1899 | H | 8ft. 0in. wide |
| 1436 | 8 | 10 | Covered Goods | 1920-1923 | H | 10 ton version of Diagram 1433 |
| 1457 | - | 10 | Covered Goods | Rebuilt 1935 (Ex-Cattle Wagon) | W | **See Chapter 5** |
| 1471 | 11 | 8 or 9 | Refrigerated Goods | circa 1898 | W | SR register states 9 ton capacity |

+ This vehicle may have been allocated SR Diagram 1432
*Some vehicles to this diagram were for poultry traffic and had Westinghouse brakes. These usually operated to and from Heathfield or Uckfield stations

The solitary rebuild of the goods brake van is something of a mystery vehicle. Southern Railway records indicate that it dates from 1876, but the reason why such a conversion of a van already nearly 50 years old was necessary eludes the authors. It is worth noting, however, that the Stroudley 7 ton vehicles were somewhat ineffective as brake vans and this might have been an experimental conversion carried out in an attempt to utilise soundly-built but otherwise redundant vehicles. Alterations included the removal of stepboards, stove and other internal fittings, and the replacement of the internal handbrake wheel by an external brake lever. In the event, the conversion remained the only one of its type, and some SR records indicate that it was scrapped in 1926 without receiving its allocated Southern number. However, at least one official source of information records the withdrawal date as December 1940, which seems highly suspect!

**Plate 44** A Stroudley-built van to LBSCR Diagram 8, officially photographed after being overhauled in November 1907, finished in the then current dark grey livery. The blue backing to the number plate shows up clearly. Notice the usual Stroudley features of single block brake, grease axleboxes and heavy self-contained buffers. Compare this with the 1882 official picture of van No. 1577 in **Plate 11**. Neither van became SR property, No. 8205 being replaced in 1913 by a new van carrying the same number. The replacement did survive into the Grouping, becoming SR No. 46553, and lasting until July 1943. Although the bodywork would have been very similar to that above, oil axleboxes and Freighter brakes were provided.

*British Rail*

**Plate 45** An equally ancient looking van to SR Diagram 1433, but one which did become SR stock. No. 01183s started life as LBSCR No. 3689 in 1891, was allocated SR number 46314 but was instead transferred to Lancing Works service stock in July 1927. It is in a hybrid SR/LBSCR departmental livery, the former LBSCR number still being visible on the wagon plate. The side louvres and roof ventilators indicate that this was once a poultry van. Note the timber brake block on one side only. The oldest poultry van extant in 1923 was SR No. 46370, built in 1880 as LBSCR No. 8014. This was scrapped in June 1927.

*E. R. Lacey*

**Plate 46** A rather more recent vehicle, LBSCR No. 8091, seen as outshopped in March 1914. A standard Diagram 1433 van, its SR number was 46446, and it survived until February 1939. Originally built in 1910 with double block brakes, it received another set on the opposite side in 1928. The original cost is recorded as a mere £69. The standard post-1911 livery shows up clearly in this official photograph.

*British Rail*

**Figure 10** A drawing of the later vans to Diagram 1433. Early vehicles had a much flatter roof profile and were therefore a few inches lower overall.

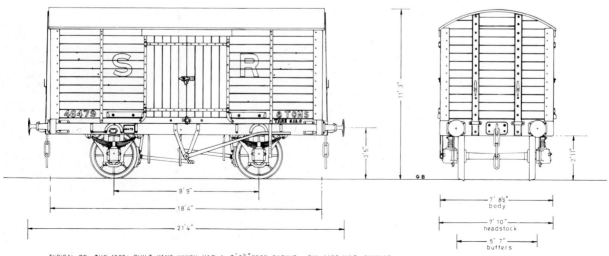

LBSC 8 TON GOODS VAN    SR DIAGRAM 1433

TYPICAL OF THE 1900s BUILT VANS WHICH HAD A 7'0¼" ROOF RADIUS. DIA.1436 WAS SIMILAR. SOME VANS HAD 4'6" SPRINGS.

**Plate 47** Although a typical van to Diagram 1433, the livery and lettering are worthy of note. LBSCR No. 8145 dates from 1910, and spent almost its entire life in departmental service, firstly as a weight-testing machine van and secondly, from 1935, as a stores van. This 1915 view clearly shows the LBSCR lettering including the 'At home in short siding Lovers Walk Brighton' legend. This exact wording also appeared in the SR service stock register so presumably was still painted on the van in Southern Railway days. The SR departmental stock number was 363s. After 1935 it was based at Streatham Hill and finally at Mitcham. The van was destroyed by enemy action on 22nd July 1944. Freighter brake gear was provided.

*British Rail*

**Plate 48** A broadside picture of SR No. 46293, formerly LBSCR No. 3632, built in 1915. The location is Bricklayers Arms in 1938. This example of Diagram 1433 has Freighter brakes and survived until July 1945; one of the last in normal traffic on the mainland.

*G. Y. Hemingway*

About 430 vans to Diagram 1433 became SR stock at the Grouping. They were by no means all identical; several variations in planking, ventilators and louvres existed, as well as the two different roof profiles already mentioned. Many entered departmental service from 1930 onwards, whilst others became a common sight as grounded stores huts, allotment huts and the like, some lasting until the 1970s in such employment. They are probably best remembered in the Isle of Wight, to where 49 vehicles of Diagrams 1433, 1434 and 1436 were transferred from 1927 onwards. Withdrawal of the Isle of Wight vans commenced in the early 1950s, but some saw out the end of steam working in December 1966.

**Plate 49** No. 1128s is a departmental van, allocated to the Chief Mechanical Engineer's use at Ashford Works in 1938, and carrying red oxide livery. The former LBSCR and SR numbers were, respectively, 8225 and 46571. It was built in 1915 and entered departmental use in July 1937.

*E. R. Lacey*

28

**Plate 50** This illustrates an Isle of Wight van to Diagram 1433, in a rather unusual pre-war SR livery, clearly indicating its restricted use. At the time, many of the vans were used for passengers' luggage in advance and, following complaints from passengers who had received fishy-smelling luggage, a few were specifically reserved for this traffic! Some carried a more symmetrical lettering layout. Van No. 46946 was equipped with Westinghouse brakes and eight brake blocks, plus being uprated to 10 tons capacity on transfer to the Island in December 1929. Its former mainland numbers were SR 46399 and LBSCR 8043. Built in 1913 it became departmental No. 549s in 1947.

*A. B. Macleod*

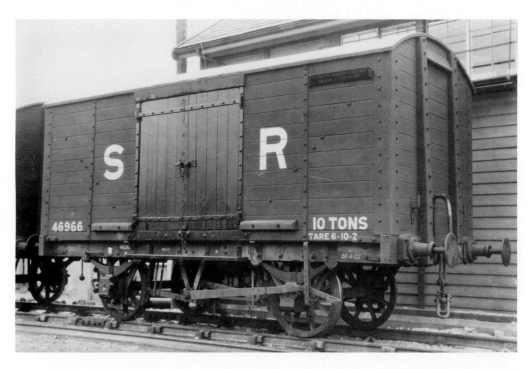

**Plate 51** Typical of the pristine condition of wagons on the Isle of Wight before 1939 is Diagram 1436 van No. 46966 shown here. This was photographed soon after transfer in May 1927, in use for passengers' luggage in advance, as stated on the board high up on the right-hand side. Some boards were simply lettered 'P.L.A.' in white on red. The stepboard under the doors was also provided specifically for this traffic. The van dates from 1920; its original LBSCR No. was 1550, the SR mainland number being 46740. Freighter brakes and a through Westinghouse pipe were provided.

*Authors' Collection*

**Plate 52** Typical of the later survivors is No. DS46957, at Ryde St. John's Road in June 1957, being used as a tool van. No less than 27 of the 35 vans to Diagram 1436 went to the Island, most entering departmental use after World War II. Fifteen vans were actually returned to the mainland at this time. No. DS46957 was one which had full Westinghouse brakes with eight brake blocks (the SR 'power brake'); some merely had through pipes. This vehicle also dates from 1920, the former numbers being SR 46762 and LBSCR 3649. The long roof rainstrip was a later addition.

*R. C. Riley*

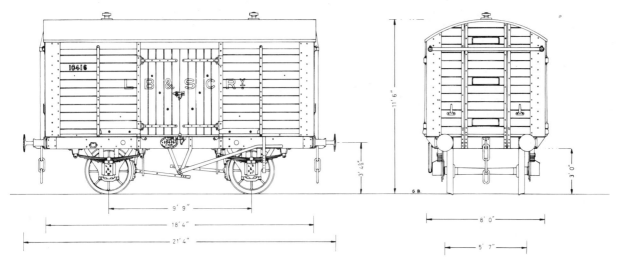

## LBSC 8 TON VAN SR DIAGRAM 1434

CONTRACTOR BUILT WITH STEEL UNDERFRAME. SOME LATER RAN ON SHORTER SPRINGS AND OIL AXLEBOXES.

**Figure 11**

During 1900/1, the Company ordered 100 steel-underframed vans from the Ashbury Carriage & Iron Company, at a cost of £175 each. Bodywork was very similar to vans built at Brighton. **Figure 11** illustrates this design.

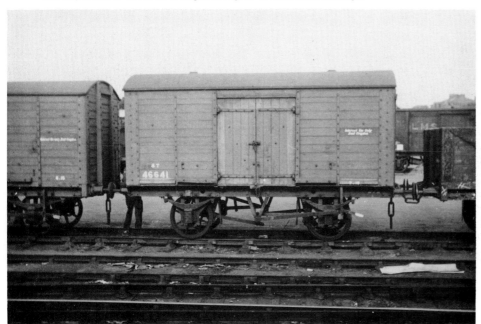

All 100 vehicles became SR property at the Grouping, although two were in departmental service by this time. LBSCR numbers were 10350-10449, of which 10379 and 10441 became service stock; the remainder were allocated SR numbers 46621-46718 in the same order. Many more entered departmental use from 1925 onwards.

**Plate 53** This shows SR No. 46641 (ex-10370) labelled 'Internal use only East Croydon', indicating that it was confined to that yard only and could not travel on the main line. Note that the 'SR' lettering was omitted at the last repaint. Double block brakes were originally fitted, these being altered to Freighter type by the time the photograph was taken, circa 1937.

*E. R. Lacey*

**Plate 54** SR Diagram 1434 was allocated to these vans. Thirteen were shipped to the Isle of Wight where they lasted until 1955. No. 46927 was photographed at St. Helens Quay in May 1953, still finished in SR postwar livery. This van received Westinghouse brakes on transfer to the Island in January 1931, the former mainland numbers being SR 46684 and LBSCR 10414. It was one of very few LBSCR vans to receive the post-1936 SR lettering style. The last survivors in ordinary traffic on the mainland were condemned in 1946.

*A. Blackburn*

**Plate 55** Well-worn pre-war SR livery is carried by this Diagram 1434 van, photographed at Godshill (IOW) in July 1952. Notice that the wagon number and almost all other lettering has been painted out, probably indicating that the vehicle was no longer in traffic. The Isle of Wight number was 46939, formerly mainland number 46694 and LBSCR No. 10424. This end view clearly shows the timber-packed steel yoke, a detail common to SR Diagrams 1371 and 1372, these being two of the other contractor-built designs on steel underframes. Provision of Westinghouse pipes dates from Isle of Wight transfer in 1931.

*A. C. Roberts*

**Plate 56** By the 1960s, few of these vans remained on rails, but one that did appears in this view , photographed at Nine Elms Wharf. Again, it is no longer in traffic and had probably not turned a wheel for many years. It also retains grease axleboxes, the initials LB&SCR being chalked over before the photograph was taken. The original number was LBSCR 10446, and it was one of 15 examples which carried experimental either-side brake gear in pre-Grouping days. In this case the Glasgow & South Western brake was provided. At a later date, this was removed and the usual double block gear was substituted, to be replaced in turn by the SR Freighter brake. The latter modification was carried out in November 1930. Details of other LBSCR either-side handbrakes are given below.

*D. J. Wigley*

### Either-side brake gear on LBSCR wagons

The LBSCR does not appear to have pursued many experiments with wagon brake gear, for the most part confining itself to single block and double brakes, the latter eventually being fitted on both sides (as in the Southern Railway's Freighter gear). However, a few vehicles were equipped experimentally with various other types of brake. Guards and shunters were instructed to keep a record of the operation of such brake gears in traffic. We presume that the experiments were either inconclusive or were unsuccessful, since none of the gears were subsequently adopted by the Company. Regrettably, the authors have been unable to locate any photographs of the vehicles concerned. The details given below are taken from the working notices dated 10th October 1915.

#### Open goods wagons

| LBSCR Number | SR Number | SR Diagram | Brake Gear Type (Date of fitting probably circa 1901-10) |
|---|---|---|---|
| 102 | 19365 | 1366 | Laycock's Improved Segmental Rack Brake |
| 103 | — | 1366 | Laycock's Patent Friction (Depending Arm) Brake |
| 104 | 19366 | 1366 | Laycock's Improved Segmental Rack Brake |
| 5825 | 24252 | 1370 | Lane's Brake Type 'A' |
| 6045 | 24446 | 1370 | Parker's Brake Type 'B' |
| 6053 | 24454 | 1370 | Great Western Brake (presumably Dean/Churchward) |
| 6133 | 24527 | 1370 | Laycock's Patent Segmental Rack Brake |

#### Covered goods wagons and brake vans

| LBSCR Number | SR Number | SR Diagram | Brake Gear Type |
|---|---|---|---|
| 10435-7 | 46705-7 | 1434 | Gresham and Craven's Brake |
| 10438-40 | 46708-10 | 1434 | McIntosh's Brake |
| 10441-3 | 46711/2 | 1434 | Stone's Brake (LBSCR No. 10441 to SR departmental No. 01064s) |
| 10444-6 | 46713-5 | 1434 | Glasgow & South Western Brake |
| 10447-9 | 46716-8 | 1434 | Froggatt's and Cock's Brake |
| 163 | 55690 | 1564 | Spencer's Brake |

It is not known at what dates these patent brake gears were removed from the wagons

## LBSC EGG TRUCK SR DIAGRAM 1435

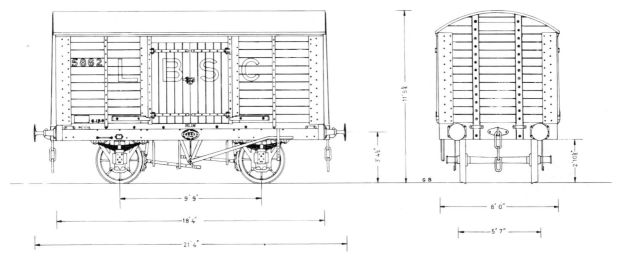

11' 5¼"

3' 4½"

2' 10½"

9' 9"

18' 4"

21' 4"

8' 0"

5' 7"

G B

THE TIMBER UNDERFRAMES HAD STEEL FLITCH PLATES.

5862 L B S C

**Figure 12** During 1898/9, twenty covered goods wagons were constructed to carry eggs in crates; this is a drawing of this design. Just why the carriage of eggs required a special design is not known but, at the time, they were the only four-wheeled 8ft. wide LBSCR goods vans. SR Diagram 1435 was allocated.

**Plate 57** This illustrates LBSCR No. 5862, later SR No. 46735, as running just after the Grouping. Double block brakes were fitted, these being altered to the Freighter type in July 1931. Withdrawal came in April 1938.

*W. O. Steel Collection*

**Figure 13**

## LBSC REFRIGERATOR VAN SR DIAGRAM 1471

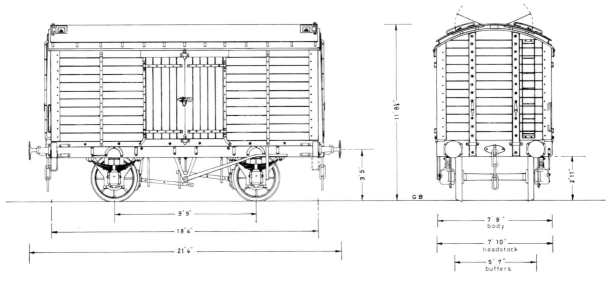

11' 8½"

3' 5"

2' 11"

9' 9"

18' 4"

21' 4"

7' 9" body

7' 10" headstock

5' 7" buffers

G B

LETTERING DETAILS NOT KNOWN

**Plate 58** The LBSCR operated very few vans for perishables traffic. A mere three vehicles were extant at the Grouping; two four wheeled vans as depicted in **Figure 13** and the solitary bogie van illustrated above.

*W. O. Steel Collection*

**Figure 13** The four wheelers date from around 1898, this being the date of the LBSCR general arrangement drawing. No photographs of them are known to exist, and neither van received its allocated SR running number, the last being scrapped in 1926. SR Diagram 1471 was allocated. What few SR records exist show the vans to have been Westinghouse-braked, yet the 1898 drawing shows them to be unfitted. There were also some discrepancies over the carrying capacities; LBSCR records state 8 tons, and the SR claim the figure to be 9 tons. It is perhaps a pity that neither van received SR livery, since this should have been stone colour with venetian red lettering; quite a contrast to the dark brown carried by other ex-LBSCR goods vans.

The bogie van, in contrast, was well documented in the contemporary railway press. Built in 1905, it spent its entire life working between Newhaven and Willow Walk, this instruction being painted on the side below the running number; 9013. The Appendix to the Service Timetable for August 1922 confirms its restricted use. LBSCR Diagram 28 was allocated and this gives the following details:

Length over headstocks..............................38ft. 0in.
Bogie centres...........................................26ft. 0in.
Length over buffers...................................41ft. 0in.
Capacity..................................................20 tons

Width over body........................................8ft. 0in.
Bogie wheelbase.......................................5ft. 6in.
Overall height..........................................11ft. 11⅜in.
Tare weight..............................19 tons 4cwt. 0qtr.

Shortly after the Grouping it was stripped of bodywork and became a 12 ton aeroplane truck. In this form it was allocated SR Diagram 1685 and running number 61072. As such, it is described in **Chapter 8**. No SR diagram or running number was allocated to the vehicle as a refrigerator van.

**Examples of numbering (for full SR numbering details refer to Appendix 1)**

| SR Diagram | SR Number | LBSCR Number | Date Built | Withdrawn | Brake Gear | Notes |
|---|---|---|---|---|---|---|
| (1432) | 46191 | 126 | 1876 | * | DB | Rebuilt from brake van in 6/23 |
| 1433 | 46221 | 1535 | 1910 | 4/46 | F | Possibly originally with DB brakes |
| 1433 | 46281 | 3612 | 1915 | 12/38 | F | To departmental No. 1374s |
| 1433 | 46311 | 3683 | 1891 | 8/32 | SL + W | Poultry van. Westinghouse brake removed 4/27 |
| 1433 | 46389 | 8033 | 1881 | 3/27 | SL + W | Poultry van. SR number not carried |
| 1433 | 46429 | 8074 | 1910 | 10/43 | DB, F 6/28 | Body grounded at Chichester 'up' Yard |
| 1433 | 46442 | 8087 | 1913 | 2/46 | F | |
| 1433 | 46537 | 8189 | 1912 | 12/45 | F | To departmental stores van No. 271s |
| 1433 | 46554 | 8206 | 1912 | 5/42 | F | Body grounded at Woking 'down' Yard |
| 1434 | 46629 | 10358 | 1900 | 2/43 | DB, F 10/32 | To departmental stores van No. 1801s |
| 1434 | 46672 | 10402 | 1900 | 10/46 | DB, F 2/31 | The last example in ordinary traffic |
| 1435 | 46720 | 5819 | 1898 | 5/41 | DB | Later with Freighter brake |
| 1435 | 46727 | 5840 | 1898 | 8/46 | DB, F 4/31 | The last example in ordinary traffic |
| 1436 | 46742 | 1582 | 1922 | 10/42 | F | |
| 1436 | 46763 | 3650 | 1920 | 11/36 | F | To internal use Woolwich Arsenal Sidings |
| 1436 | 46766 | 3655 | 1920 | 2/46 | F | One of the last in ordinary traffic |
| 1457 | 46924 | - | Reb. 1935 | 6/48 | ES + W | To departmental No. 1066s **(see Plate 63)** |
| 1471 | 50594 | 3765 | c1898 | 11/24 | See | SR number not carried |
| 1471 | 50595 | 3766 | c1898 | 7/26 | Text | SR number not carried |

\* See text for explanation
For numbering of Isle of Wight Transfers see **Appendix 1**

# Chapter 5
## Livestock Vehicles

Four hundred and twenty ordinary cattle wagons were in service at the Grouping, plus a further twenty nine special cattle vans used for the conveyance of prize stock. The ordinary vehicles were all very similar; indeed the LBSCR allocated just one diagram to them, No. 12. The Southern Railway separated them into pre and post-1919 construction, the main difference concerning carrying capacity. The earlier wagons were rated at 6 tons, and the later ones at 10 tons. Constructionally, however, they were almost identical, the later vehicles being 1½ in. wider over corner pillars. In 1938, all remaining 10 ton vehicles were downrated to 6 tons capacity. Southern Railway diagram numbers were 1527 (6 tons) and 1528 (10 tons). Six

wagons were transferred to the Isle of Wight in 1927, and three of these became the last survivors of the type, being withdrawn in 1955. The other three were reconstructed as covered goods wagons in 1935 to SR Diagram 1457, and are discussed briefly in **Chapter 4.** They are illustrated here as the modifications were hardly extensive, and it was thought better to deal with them in this section, so that a direct comparison with the original vehicles could be obtained. One of these conversions remains in existence today, as the sole surviving LBSCR cattle wagon. At the time of writing, it is in the custody of the Wight Locomotive Society, on permanent loan from the National Railway Museum.

**Plate 59** This 1882 official picture shows a typical early cattle wagon of 6 tons capacity, to J. C. Craven's specification. It has rather elaborate timber body framing and an iron underframe. The number is 1786, but this and virtually all other trace of livery have been obliterated by limewash. It is doubtful if many wagons of this type remained in service after 1900. None were in traffic by 1910.

*British Rail*

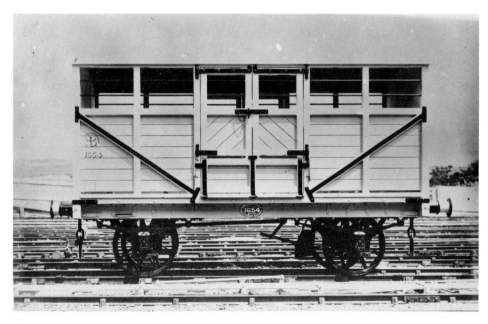

**Plate 60** Another official photograph, taken in 1882, depicting Stroudley cattle wagon No. 1654, clearly in ex-works condition. This design remained virtually unaltered for the rest of the LBSCR's existence. Apart from buffers, brake gear and axleboxes, the final vehicles built in 1922 were practically identical. Billinton introduced the slightly higher roof profile at the same time as this modification was applied to the covered goods wagons, thought to have been around the mid-1890s. Wagon No. 1654 did not survive at the Grouping, at least not in the form illustrated, since a replacement cattle wagon bearing the same number was built in 1906 at a cost of £79. This vehicle ran until 1930, becoming SR No. 52934 to Diagram 1527. The oldest of these wagons extant at the Grouping dated from 1886, and the most recent from 1917.

*British Rail*

**Plate 61** LBSCR No. 7479 dates from 1912 and was two years old when photographed. It subsequently became SR No. 53172 and was condemned in May 1930 after a relatively short working life of 18 years. This was typical of many cattle wagons since the growth of refrigerated meat trade, many going for scrap long before they were life-expired. However, a few LBSCR examples managed to survive on the mainland until just after nationalisation. It should also be pointed out that the three Isle of Wight survivors hardly turned a wheel after World War II, despite being painted in British Railways unfitted light grey livery soon after 1948. Incidentally, this livery was in fact incorrect, as all three were Westinghouse-braked or piped. Isle of Wight livery practice often varied from that on the mainland, even during BR days.

*British Rail*

## L B S C  6 TON  CAT TLE  WAGON  S R DIAGRAM 1527

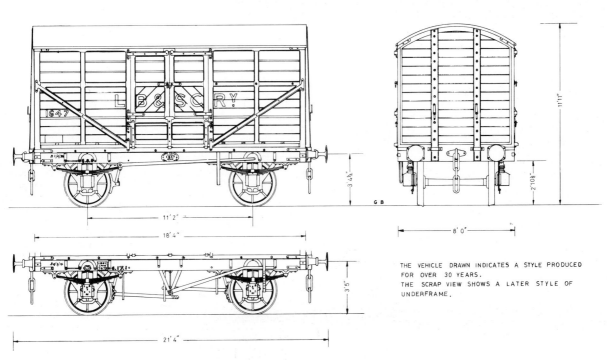

THE VEHICLE DRAWN INDICATES A STYLE PRODUCED
FOR OVER 30 YEARS.
THE SCRAP VIEW SHOWS A LATER STYLE OF
UNDERFRAME.

**Figure 14**  A drawing of the cattle wagon to SR Diagram 1527.

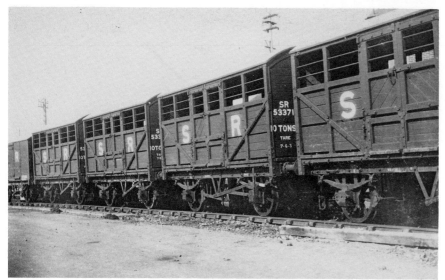

**Plate 62** Four of the six Isle of Wight cattle wagons are visible in this 1927 picture. Official records state that all were to SR Diagram 1528, yet not all appear to have the wider corner pillars characteristic of the final twenty wagons, so it may be that some to Diagram 1527 were shipped across instead. However, all are recorded as being of 10 tons capacity. Note the two variations in brake gear; Freighter with Westinghouse pipe on No. 53371, full Westinghouse with power brake on the others. No Diagram 1528 cattle wagons were Westinghouse-braked on the mainland, but 35 vehicles to Diagram 1527 were so equipped in LBSCR days, enabling them to run in passenger trains. Most of these had vacuum pipes added after the Grouping and, in time, also lost their Westinghouse brakes. It is possible that these were removed in order to equip the covered goods and cattle wagons destined for the Isle of Wight, since the dates correspond fairly closely.

*A. B. Macleod*

**Plate 63** Livestock traffic declined on the Isle of Wight in the mid-1930s, and the six vehicles were clearly unnecessary. Three were modified in 1935 as covered goods wagons. This photograph illustrates the last survivor, in departmental service at Newport (IOW) in 1963. By then numbered 1066s, the former traffic department number has been roughly painted on. Indeed, there seems to be no other trace of paint on the vehicle! Built in 1922 as LBSCR No. 7116, it was allocated SR mainland number 53291, but went instead to the Isle of Wight, receiving the number 53374. On conversion to Diagram 1457, it was renumbered as 46924, finally entering departmental stock in 1948. The method of conversion to a covered goods wagon may be easily deduced from the photograph. It is this vehicle which is now preserved on the Isle of Wight.

*M. Lockett*

General withdrawal of LBSCR cattle wagons on the mainland took place during the 1930s, and only a small number remained after World War II. At least one wagon to Diagram 1527 was sold to the Hundred of Manhood and Selsey Tramway, one of Colonel Stephen's light railways, and this survived until the tramway closed in 1935.

### Examples of numbering (for full SR numbering details refer to Appendix 1)

| SR Diagram | SR Number | LBSCR Number | Date Built | Withdrawn | Brake Gear | Notes | SR Diagram | SR Number | LBSCR Number | Date Built | Withdrawn | Brake Gear |
|---|---|---|---|---|---|---|---|---|---|---|---|---|
| 1527 | 52915 | 1634 | 6/08 | 2/46 | SL + W | 1 | 1527 | 53205 | 7555 | 6/11 | 9/50 | F |
| 1527 | 52934 | 1698 | 6/07 | 8/33 | SL + W | 2 | 1528 | 53286 | 4049 | 6/22 | 3/51 | F |
| 1527 | 53018 | 7209 | 12/12 | 9/50 | F | | 1528 | 53292 | 7117 | 6/22 | 6/47 | F |
| 1527 | 53095 | 7396 | 1886 | 7/23 | SB | | 1528 | 53301 | 7559 | 6/22 | 7/48 | F |

Notes: 1. Altered to Westinghouse pipe only in 1927; Freighter brake fitted in 1928.
2. Altered to Westinghouse pipe only in 1927; Freighter brake fitted in November 1930.
For numbering of Isle of Wight transfers see **Appendix 1**.

Three batches of special cattle vans were completed by the LBSCR. The first two were very similar to the goods wagons, but the final design was really a passenger van, and these were numbered in the passenger stock series when built. The others were reclassified and renumbered similarly about 1923. In the same manner as the goods cattle wagons, the LBSCR considered the first two types as one, and allocated just one diagram. The Southern Railway allocated each batch a different diagram number, both these and the SR running numbers being in the passenger van series. Details of the vehicles are as follows:

| SR Diagram | LBSCR Diagram | Capacity (Tons) | Length over Headstocks | Wheelbase | Date Built | LBSCR Goods Stock Nos. | LBSCR Pass. Stock Nos. | SR Nos. | Remarks |
|---|---|---|---|---|---|---|---|---|---|
| 1059 | 13 | 8** | 18ft. 0in. | 11ft. 0in. | 1892 | 7161-72 | 533-44 | 3820-31 | All withdrawn in 1931 |
| 1060 | 13 | 8** | 18ft. 4in. | 11ft. 2in. | 1894 | 7173-84 | 545-55 | 3832-42 | No. 7182 withdrawn in 6/1921; all others withdrawn in 1931 |
| 1061 | 14 | 9 | 20ft. 0in. | 11ft. 6in. | 6/21 | 7971-6* | 527-32 | 3843-8 | Nos. 3844/8 withdrawn in 1952 |

** Some copies of LBSCR Diagram 13 state the capacity as 4 tons.
* These 6 vehicles were authorised in 1915 and were originally allocated goods stock numbers. These numbers were never carried by the vans.
All vans had Westinghouse brakes and through vacuum pipes.

**Plate 64** The special cattle vans seem to have been missed by the photographers. The only view of the earlier designs known to the authors is reproduced here. This is in a general view of Hailsham Station, probably dating from the first decade of this century. No trace of lettering is visible, and it is considered most likely that they carried passenger van livery between 1892 and 1923. One contemporary observer describes the vehicles as 'cattle trucks fitted and painted to run in passenger trains' but recorded no further details. The vans may never have carried their allocated LBSCR passenger stock numbers, since reclassification did not take place until just before the Grouping.

*Authors' Collection*

**Figure 15**   This depicts the 1894 design; later allocated SR Diagram 1060.

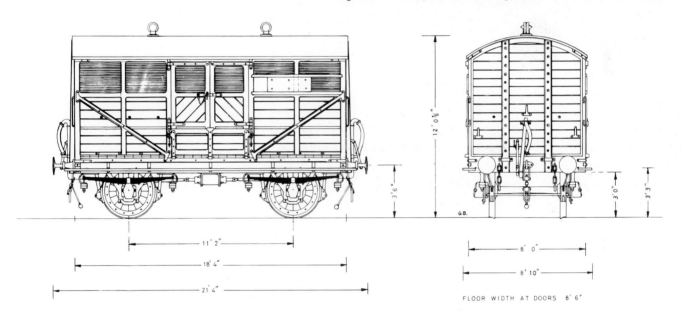

11' 2"

18' 4"

21' 4"

12' 0⅝"

3' 6"

8' 0"

8' 10"

3' 0"

3' 3"

G.B.

FLOOR WIDTH AT DOORS 8' 6"

# LBSC CATTLE BOX-AIR BRAKED   SR DIAGRAM 1060

**Plate 65** Diagram 1061 special cattle van No. 3848 as running in 1947, still sporting the pre-war Southern livery of dark green with yellow lettering and black ends. Notice the provision of a drover's compartment, and the similarity with contemporary horse-box designs. Spoke wheels were originally fitted. The van is branded 'LOAD 8 TONS' yet SR registers state this to be 9 tons. Formerly LBSCR No. 532, it was one of the two vehicles which remained in service until 1952, finally being replaced by a batch of special cattle vans built to a Southern Railway design of 1930. The vehicle on the right is an ex-SECR special cattle van.

*Authors' Collection*

# Chapter 6
## Goods Brake Vans

Other groups of LBSCR wagons might lack variety, but the same cannot be said of the goods brake vans, no less than sixteen Southern Railway diagrams being allocated. In several cases, these differentiated between otherwise identical vans with tare weights of 7, 8, 9, 10 and 12 tons, but despite this, at least nine varieties may be identified. They range from somewhat antiquated Stroudley vehicles, of as little as 7 tons tare, up to modern long wheelbase 20 ton vans on steel underframes, the latter dating from 1922. The Southern Railway completed several more of these vans during 1923, and then proceeded to rebuild over half of them into ballast brakes, in which form several survived into the 1980s, in marked contrast to most other LBSCR stock.

The Stroudley vans came in several versions, there being two widths and at least two different roof profiles. All were provided with side doors and could be termed 'Road' vans (see **Volume One** for an explanation of this term). A few also had a lantern look-out in the roof, but no mention of this appears on post-1910 LBSCR diagrams, and it would seem that this feature was dispensed with at an earlier date. Others had heavy cast-iron headstocks and brake blocks fitted in an attempt to increase the tare weight to a reasonably useful figure. By the Grouping, these vans were completely outclassed. A 1920 pro-

posal to couple them in pairs under the control of one guard was not judged a success, and after one more was converted to a covered goods van, it was left to the Southern Railway to withdraw them practically en bloc during 1924, without even renumbering them. Several others were already in departmental service by this time, and lasted a little longer. Perhaps, surprisingly, the final survivor was retained in Engineers' use until September 1938 **(see Plate 69)**. The covered goods rebuild is discussed on **page 26.**

Robert Billinton favoured vehicles with verandas at each end and built 9, 10 and 12 ton versions of this design, plus a six-wheeled 20 tonner. None of these had side doors giving direct access into the guard's compartment, and so could not be used as 'Road' vans. A. H. Panter continued to build these vans but produced some four and six-wheeled road vans in the World War 1 period, the bodywork of which resembled his father's LSWR design of 30 years earlier. Finally, he built the modern long wheelbase 20 ton design referred to above. This vehicle appeared too late to be allocated an LBSCR diagram number.

The following list details all the Southern Railway diagram numbers allocated to these vehicles, and also includes the post-Grouping rebuild of the Panter 1922 vans.

| SR Diagram | LBSCR Diagram | Tare* (Tons) | Body Dimensions<br>Length, Width, Height from Rail | Wheelbase | Known Construction Period | Remarks |
|---|---|---|---|---|---|---|
| 1564 | 21 | 7 | 16ft. 0in. x 7ft. 7¼ in. x 10ft. 5¾in. | 9ft. 9in. | 1872-1889 | Standard Stroudley 'Road' van |
| 1757 | 21 | 8 | As Diagram 1564 | As D1564 | As Diagram 1564 | Allocated to Engineer's Dept. |
| 1570 | — | 7 each | As Diagram 1564 | As D1564 | Converted 1923 | Two D1564 vans close-coupled |
| 1565 | 33 | 7 | 16ft. 0in. x 7ft. 7¼ in. x 11ft. 0in. | 9ft. 9in. | 1878/1882 | As D1564, sharper roof radius |
| 1567 | 27 | 9 | 16ft. 0in. x 7ft. 5½ in. x 10ft. 5¾in. | 9ft. 9in. | 1888-1890 | Narrower version of D1564 |
| 1569 | 27 | 10 | As Diagram 1567 | As D1567 | As Diagram 1567 | 10 ton version of D1567 |
| 1571 | — | 10 each | As Diagram 1567 | As D1567 | Converted 1923 | Two D1569 vans close-coupled |
| 1566 | 22 | 9 | 16ft. 0in. x 7ft. 9in. x 11ft. 8½in. | 9ft. 9in. | 1894 | Standard Billinton vehicle |
| 1568 | 22 | 10 | As Diagram 1566 | As D1566 | 1894-1907 | 10 ton version of D1566 |
| 1572 | 22 | 12 | As Diagram 1566 | As D1566 | 1895-1908 | 12 ton version of D1566 |
| 1575 | 23 | 20 | 16ft. 0in. x 8ft. 0in. x 11ft. 10in. | 5ft. + 5ft. | 1900-1902 | Six-wheeled Billinton design |
| 1573 | 34 | 15 | 15ft. 5in. x 7ft. 9in. | 9ft. 3in. | 1907 | Shunting truck/incline brake |
| 1574 | 24 | 15 | 18ft. 0in. x 8ft. 0in. x 11ft. 8in. | 10ft. 6in. | 1915-1916 | Panter 'Road' van design |
| 1577 | 25 | 20 | 20ft. 0in. x 8ft. 0in. x 11ft. 8in. | 5ft. 9in. + 5ft. 9in. | 1915-1916 | Panter six-wheeled 'Road' van |
| 1576 | — | 20 | 24ft. 0in. x 8ft. 0in. x 11ft. 9in. | 16ft. 0in. | 1922-1923 | Some completed by SR. Most were rebuilt to D1760 in 1928/9/37 |
| 1760 | — | 20 | Steel Underframe<br>As Diagram 1576 | As D1576 | Rebuilt 1928/9/37 | Rebuilt from D1576 vans |

*\* Tare weights often varied from the official figure*

The solitary incline brake van appears to have been built on an ordinary wagon underframe, being little more than a flat wagon with a centrally-mounted brake standard and handrails all round. It was used at Brighton Lower Yard, which was approached via a steep incline. Although allocated SR brake van number 55863 in 1925, it was reallocated the number 61361 in the miscellaneous wagons part of the list, along with the other shunting trucks and similar vehicles. Neither SR number appears to have been carried, as the wagon was scrapped in 1927 still numbered as LBSCR 326.

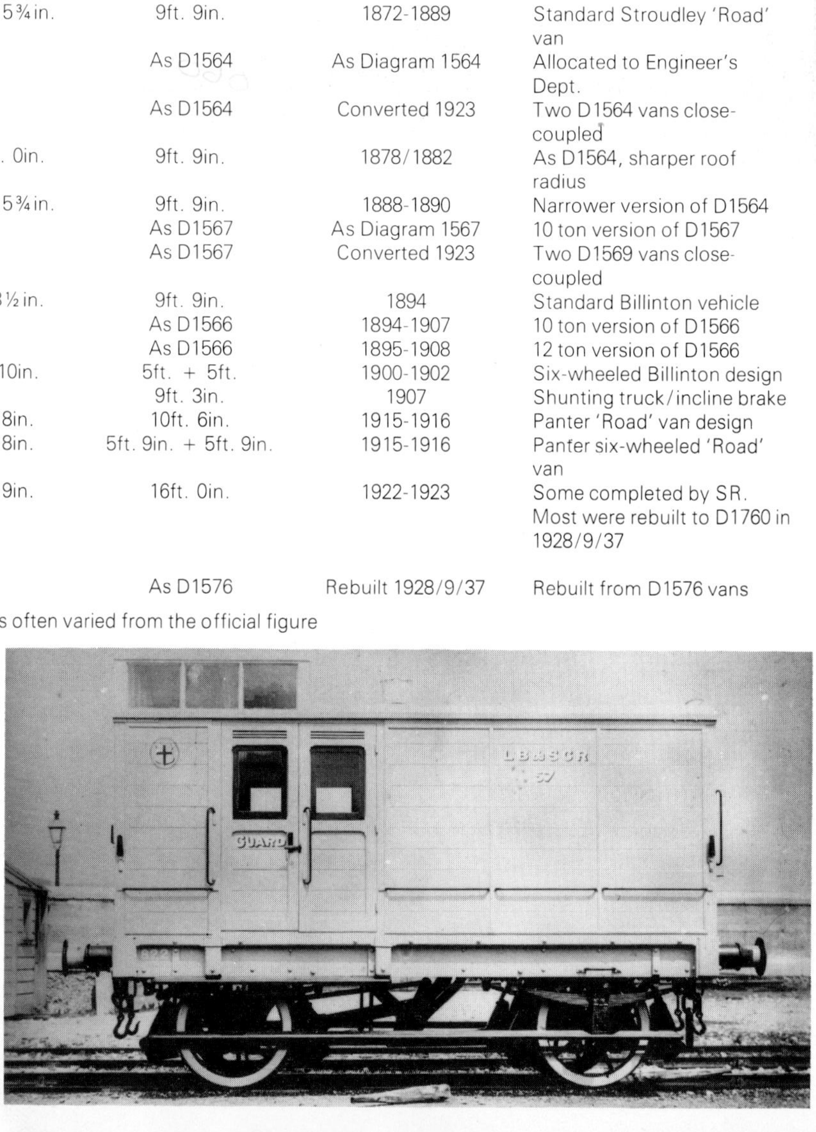

**Plate 66** This 1882 picture shows brake van No. 57 when built, complete with lantern look-out and oil lighting. It should be noted that end steps and a roof handrail were provided — details that were absent from similar vans without raised look-outs. Notice also that both the 'illiterate' symbol and the Company initials are carried. This van survived until August 1924 and was allocated SR number 55626. By this date the lantern look-out had been removed.

*British Rail*

**Plate 67** Van No. 104, an 1873 Stroudley vehicle, photographed in dark grey livery in 1907. Completed at a cost of £275, it remained in service until 1924. It was among the oldest wagons to be taken over by the SR, finishing its days as duplicate No. 0104. The SR number, 55643, was allocated but not carried. Of the 357 LBSCR brake vans passed to the Southern, no less than 167 were Stroudley vehicles, similar to the ones illustrated on this page. Apart from the omission of the lantern look-out, there appears to be very little difference from van No. 57 in **Plate 66**. Several vans were sold to the Isle of Wight companies, details of which may be found in **Chapter 11**.

*British Rail*

**Plate 68** This interesting picture shows van No. 196 at East Croydon in the spring of 1912, bearing an overhaul date of 7/7/11. It is the earliest dated photograph of a wagon carrying the final style of Company lettering, viz. LBSC and not LBSCR. It is also the only definitely recorded use of the 10½ in. initials referred to on **page 7**. Note that the door is still labelled 'Guard'. The van itself is a standard Diagram 1564 type, and was built in 1882, part of a batch supplied by the Midland Railway Carriage & Wagon Company. The SR number, 55716, was allocated but, as usual, was never carried.

*L. E. Brailsford*

**Figure 16** A drawing of the most common version of Stroudley 'Road' brake van. Vans with lantern look-outs did not have end windows in the bodywork.

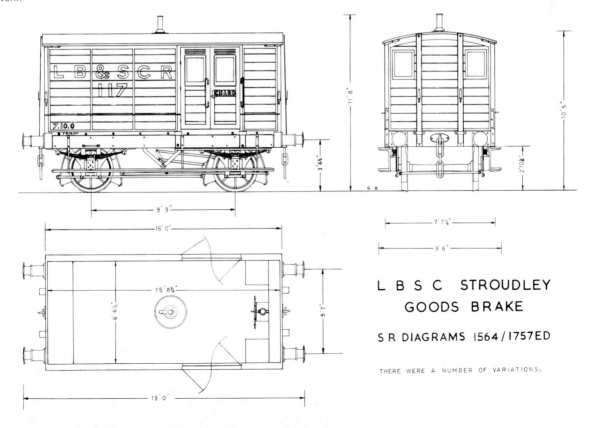

L B S C STROUDLEY
GOODS BRAKE

S R DIAGRAMS 1564 / 1757 ED

THERE WERE A NUMBER OF VARIATIONS.

**Plate 69** A few Stroudley brake vans were permanently allocated to the Engineer's Department for ballast train work. In pre-Grouping days, these carried the word 'Ballast' in large letters on the bodyside. Only three became SR Engineer's property, being allocated Diagram 1757. Two were condemned in 1927 but the last, No. 62823, survived for another eleven years, finally being scrapped in September 1938. This view depicts this sole survivor in ED livery of red oxide, at West Croydon in March 1935. Built in 1886, the former LBSCR number was 48.

*H. F. Wheeller*

**Plate 70** Billinton goods brake No. 264, complete with black shading to the lettering and Company initials LB&SCRᵞ, as used from about 1899 until 1903. The shading was unusual but by no means unknown. Built in 1899, this vehicle became SR No. 55809 to Diagram 1568, and ran until September 1931. It was rated at 10 tons, but there were identical vans with tare weights of around 9 tons and 12 tons. General withdrawal of these brake vans took place in the early 1930s, as ex-LSWR road vans were drafted in to replace LBSCR and SECR small vans on branch line and local trip workings. Nevertheless, a few survived World War II and the last, SR No. 55781, was scrapped in May 1947. No. 264 is pictured at Havant.

*W. O. Steel Collection*

**Figure 17** This shows one of the two styles of brake rodding fitted to these vehicles. Compare this with the van in **Plate 72**.

## LBSC 10 & 12 TON GOODS BRAKE VAN

### SR DIAGRAM 1568

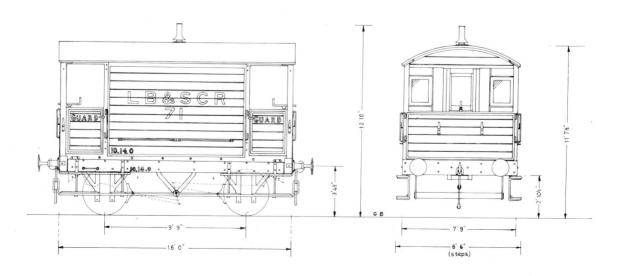

On 9th September 1904, D1 class 0-4-2 tank No. 239 *Patcham* was derailed at Cocking, on the Chichester to Midhurst branch. Goods brake van No. 260 was also damaged, as seen in **Plate 71**. Details of the veranda end and roof construction are revealed. Notice that the cast-iron headstock also includes the brake standard housing in the casting. Built in 1898, van No. 260 survived the accident and became SR No. 55805, to Diagram 1568 and was withdrawn in June 1930. The lettering layout is usual for the 1903-11 period. Attention is drawn to the wine bottle just to the left of the brake standard!

*Authors' Collection*

**Plate 72** The 12 ton vans were allocated SR Diagram 1572. One of these, SR No. 55856, is seen at West Croydon in March 1930. This was formerly LBSCR No. 265, and it was built in 1899 at a cost of £154. Condemned in February 1938, it was then the last surviving Billinton 12 ton van in ordinary traffic. One more, No. 55850, was returned to traffic department use in September 1938 after a period in service stock, during which time it carried the number 906s. It had acquired vacuum pipes in June 1936, and ran until condemned in June 1943. Note the brake rodding details on van No. 55856. This has eight brake blocks; Nos. 260 and 264 have only four blocks.

*H. F. Wheeller*

**Plate 73** Although the last 10 ton Billinton brake van was withdrawn from ordinary traffic in 1947, it was not the last in existence. Van No. 55829 (ex-LBSCR No. 301 of 1902) was withdrawn in August 1945, and was subsequently adapted by the Civil Engineer's Department as a gauging van, as seen here. In this form, it survived into the 1950s, but for some reason failed to receive a departmental stock number. The two lengths of diagonal strapping forming an inverted 'vee' on the body side pre-date the 1945 conversion, and were a common addition to these vans in early SR days. In the same way as LSWR Diagram 1541 brake vans were allocated specific duties, so were several vans to Diagram 1568. Some examples may be found on **page 48**.

*Lens of Sutton*

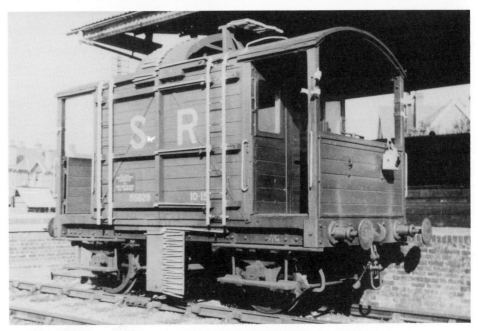

**Plate 74** Billinton's final brake van design was a 20 ton six-wheeled version of the standard type. Twenty were built by contractors in 1900-2 and nineteen became SR property, allocated to Diagram 1575. This photograph illustrates one in SR pre-1936 livery, taken about 1934. No. 55893 was built in 1902 and survived until June 1943, being among the last of the type to remain in service.

*E. R. Lacey*

**Plate 75** Van No. 55893 again, seen at Purley in June 1937. Since the view in **Plate 74** was photographed, the vehicle has received a 'Not to work between Tonbridge and West St. Leonards via Battle' board, and the side lamp irons have been repositioned higher up the corner pillars. These 20 ton vans were 3in. wider than other Billinton brakes, hence the restriction on travelling over the Hastings line. These brake vans seldom ran off the Central Division, and in June 1935 all were based at Norwood Yard, this fact being stencilled on the van sides. Also visible in this picture is a Southern Railway 25 ton brake van.

*E. R. Lacey*

Numbering details of Diagram 1575 are as follows:

| LBSCR Numbers | SR Numbers | Built by |
|---|---|---|
| 273-284 | 55878-88* | Cravens, 1900/1 |
| 303-310 | 55889-96 | Birmingham RC&W Co. 1902 |

*LBSCR No. 280 was scrapped before the Grouping

**Plate 76 (Right)** Robert Billinton's 10 and 12 ton vans continued to be built until the end of 1908, and it was not until 1915 that A. H. Panter designed his own vehicles. Two of these were outside-framed 'Road' vans, the prototypes of which were completed in December 1915. Both were officially photographed, the lighter vehicle being illustrated opposite. LBSCR No. 348 later became SR No. 55864, running until May 1946. The cost when new was £275. Notice the similarity with LSWR brake vans; clearly William Panter provided the inspiration for these designs.

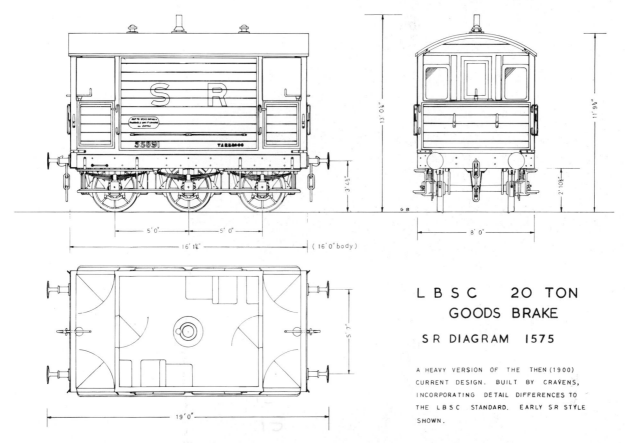

### LBSC 20 TON GOODS BRAKE

### SR DIAGRAM 1575

A HEAVY VERSION OF THE THEN (1900) CURRENT DESIGN. BUILT BY CRAVENS, INCORPORATING DETAIL DIFFERENCES TO THE LBSC STANDARD. EARLY SR STYLE SHOWN.

**Plate 76** Note the absence of 'orange-red' ends.

*British Rail*

**Figure 18** This depicts the 20 ton Billinton van. In pre-Grouping days, these vans would have been rostered for heavy main line goods services.

**Plate 77** Diagram 1574, van No. 55866, at Stewarts Lane in 1935. The wagon number and tare appear to have been freshly repainted, in marked contrast to the worn Company initials. Such partial repainting was a very common practice and became the rule rather than the exception after 1939. Built as LBSCR No. 350 in 1916, it ran until June 1945. Several of these vehicles received through steam and vacuum pipes in the 1930s, enabling them to run in branch line mixed trains.

*G. Y. Hemingway*

**Plate 78** This delightful picture shows van No. 55865 being shunted at Lyme Regis by Adams radial tank No. 3520 in August 1937. It has received vacuum and steam pipes, plus screw couplings, and regularly ran in the branch passenger train. Both types of Panter road brake vans were well received by South Western Section goods train guards, almost certainly because of their similarity with ex-LSWR brake vans. In general, apart from the three A. H. Panter designs, ex-LBSCR brake vans were a rare sight in the West Country. Diagram 1574 vehicles were the most common on LSWR branch lines, and the authors have photographic evidence of these vans, at Wadebridge in the 1930s, and at Sidmouth in the 1940s. General withdrawal of this diagram took place between 1944 and 1950 (see **page 45** for numbering details). These vehicles are depicted in **Figure 19**.

*F. Foote*

**Figure 19**

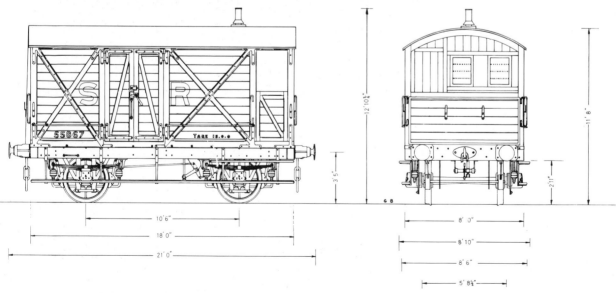

## LBSC 15 TON GOODS BRAKE
### SR DIAGRAM 1574

44

THIS DESIGN WAS VERY SIMILAR TO A TYPE ALREADY
IN USE ALL OVER THE LSWR SYSTEM.
THE INTERNAL PARTITIONS WERE REMOVED, SOME
BEFORE SR DAYS. SEE D.1577 FOR OTHER END.

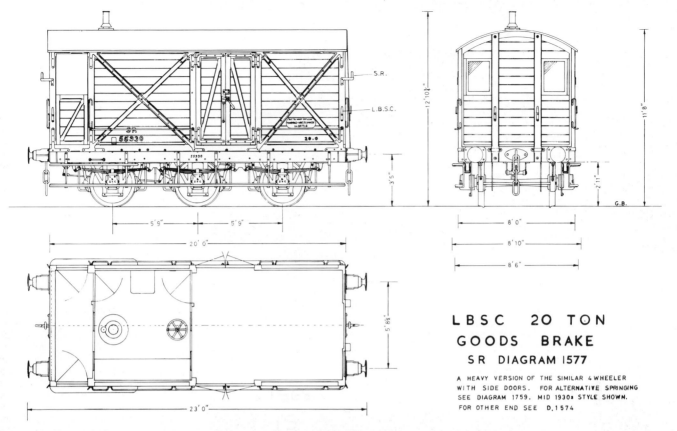

S.R.

L.B.S.C.

12'10½"

11'8"

3'5"

2'11"

G.B.

5'9"    5'9"

20'0"

8'0"

8'10"

8'6"

5'8½"

23'0"

## LBSC 20 TON GOODS BRAKE
### SR DIAGRAM 1577

A HEAVY VERSION OF THE SIMILAR 4 WHEELER WITH SIDE DOORS. FOR ALTERNATIVE SPRINGING SEE DIAGRAM 1759. MID 1930s STYLE SHOWN. FOR OTHER END SEE D.1574

**Figure 20**   This illustrates the heavier six-wheeled road van design of 1915.

**Plate 79**   The official picture of 20 ton van No. 333; the family likeness with No. 348 is obvious. Van No. 333 became SR No. 55928 and was scrapped in July 1947; SR Diagram 1577 was allocated. The cost of one van was originally £340. Note the employment of disc wheels; a rare fitting on LBSCR wagons before about 1920.

*British Rail*

Numbering details of the two Panter 'Road' vans are as follows:

| SR Diagram | LBSCR Nos. | SR Nos. |
| --- | --- | --- |
| 1574 | 348-361 | 55864-77 |
| 1577 | 333-347 | 55928-42 |

All were built at Lancing Works and were charged to the capital as opposed to the renewal account.

**Plate 80**   Van No. 55935 at Kingston in 1935. Interworking of heavy brake vans (ie. 20 tons and over) between each division, in the London area at least, was not uncommon by the mid-1930s. This particular example was scrapped in February 1945. General withdrawal of these vehicles took place between 1944 and circa 1950, but No. 55937 was condemned much earlier, in March 1933.

*J. W. Sparrowe*

Panter's final goods brake van design was for a 20 ton long wheel-base vehicle on a steel underframe, considerably superior to any previous LBSCR brake van. In fact this was the last new LBSCR wagon design to appear before the Grouping, failing to receive an LBSCR diagram number. The introduction of these wagons was well covered by the contemporary railway press, so evidently the Company was proud of its new additions to the goods fleet. A total of twenty was completed in 1922, with a further eleven early in 1923. All appear to have entered service carrying LBSCR numbers, but possibly the last ones were finished in SR livery but retaining their pre-Grouping numbers, in the style depicted in **Plate 26**. The original cost was £802 per vehicle, which compares very favourably with contemporary LSWR brake vans.

There is no doubt that the LBSCR were slow in providing heavy brake vans, and the Company's working notices regularly instructed that two brake vans were to be provided on the majority of main line goods trains, usually one at the front and another at the rear, but on some services both could be attached to the rear of the train. Whilst this was essential with vans of as little as 7 tons tare, it was undoubtedly wasteful of manpower since both vehicles had to be provided with a goods guard. Some of the steeply-graded branch lines also required the provision of two brake vans.

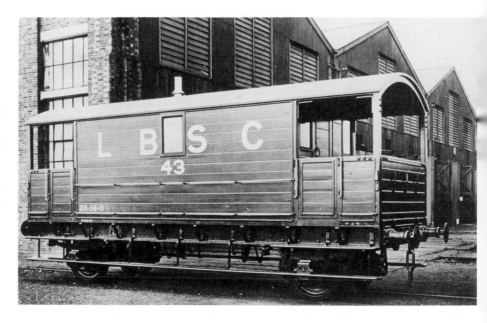

**Plate 81** Brake van No. 43, as outshopped from Lancing Works in September 1922. Later allocated the SR number 55898, it remained in the condition shown until 1937 when it was rebuilt into a ballast brake van. As such it features again in **Plate 84.** SR Diagram 1576 was allocated in 1923, this being amended to 1760 on rebuilding.
*British Rail*

**Plate 82** Some vans had the bottom planks covered by steel sheeting, typified by No. 55915 as running in 1948. This was built in 1923 but it is not known when the steel sheeting was added. The former LBSCR number was 381. Note the heavy self-contained buffers and the alternative position of the side lamp irons. Post-1936 lettering is carried, but the former style is still visible.

*E. B. Trotter*

**Plate 83** Just two of these brake vans failed to enter British Railways stock in 1948. One of these was No. 55918, seen at Three Bridges in August 1946 still in pre-1936 livery. It was condemned in November 1947. After 1937 there were only 14 of the original 31 vehicles remaining in traffic department use; the rest had been rebuilt as ballast brake vans, in the form illustrated on **page 48**.

*R. E. Tustin*

**Figure 21** This depicts the original 1922 design.

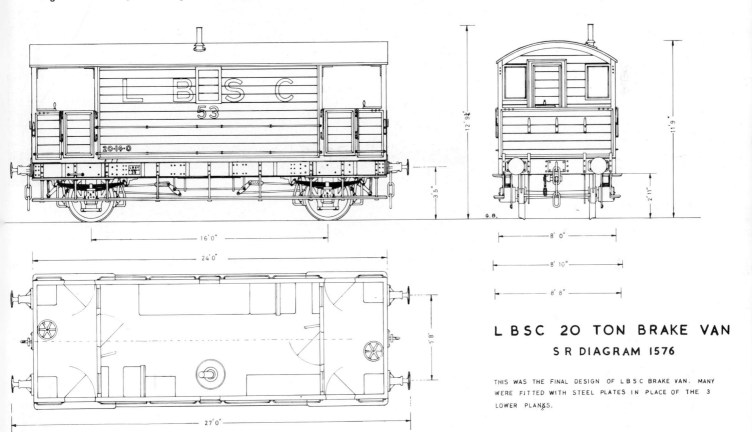

L B S C   2 0   T O N   B R A K E   V A N

S R   D I A G R A M   1 5 7 6

THIS WAS THE FINAL DESIGN OF L B S C BRAKE VAN. MANY WERE FITTED WITH STEEL PLATES IN PLACE OF THE 3 LOWER PLANKS.

Occasionally, these vans were allocated to specific yards, SR No. 55912 being based at New Cross Gate in 1947. No. 55921 was curiously labelled 'STOCKHOLM' at the same date.

The last survivor in an unrebuilt state was No. DS55907, which entered departmental service in April 1960 and was retained until 1971. During this period it could normally be found at Three Bridges and served as a brake van for a mobile generator train. This train comprised four interesting vehicles; the others being an SECR utility van, an SR 12 ton covered goods wagon and an LSWR brake van to Diagram 1541.

The seventeen rebuilds were quite extensively modified, losing one veranda in the process. As Engineer's Department vehicles some have survived until the 1980s, most being transferred to other regions of BR since the mid-1970s. As such, they are the last ex-LBSCR wagons to serve with British Rail outside the Isle of Wight. Details of the rebuildings are as below.

| D1760 No. | D1576 No. | Date | D1760 No. | D1576 No. | Date | D1760 No. | D1576 No. | Date |
|---|---|---|---|---|---|---|---|---|
| 62840 | 55899 | 8/28 | 62846 | 55910 | 1/29 | 62852 | 55903 | 4/37 |
| 62841 | 55916 | 1/29 | 62847 | 55898 | 3/37 | 62853 | 55925 | 5/37 |
| 62842 | 55920 | 9/28 | 62848 | 55900 | 3/37 | 62854 | 55902 | 6/37 |
| 62843 | 55922 | 9/28 | 62849 | 55913 | 4/37 | 62855 | 55909 | 12/37 |
| 62844 | 55924 | 9/28 | 62850 | 55914 | 4/37 | 62856 | 55917 | 12/37 |
| 62845 | 55905 | 1/29 | 62851 | 55906 | 4/37 | | | |

The conversions were carried out under SR order Nos. L341 (dated June 1928), L382 (dated September 1928) and A941 (dated September 1936).

**Plate 84** The same van as featured in **Plate 81,** but in its new guise as a ballast brake van. It was photographed about 1950. This was the first of the 1937 conversions and survived until December 1958. Note that vacuum brakes have been added. Most of the rebuilds to Diagram 1760 served on the Central and South Eastern divisions, but at least one was based at Broad Clyst (LSWR) in the early 1960s.

*Lens of Sutton*

**Plate 85** A similar vehicle, No. S62844, appears at Three Bridges in July 1949. This was one of the original 1928 rebuilds and has steel sheeting over the lower side planks. The method of conversion may be deduced by comparison with **Figure 21**. These ballast brakes could run over the Tonbridge to Hastings line, unlike the original design. The side sheeting and side lamp irons were inset to allow sufficient clearance. Van No. 62844 remained in Engineer's Department use until June 1955. Notice the provision of end steps to allow access to the lamp tops on the roof.

*Lens of Sutton*

**Examples of numbering (for full details of SR numbering refer to Appendix 1)**

| SR Diagram | SR Number | LBSCR Number | Date Built | With-drawn | Notes | SR Diagram | SR Number | LBSCR Number | Date Built | With-drawn | Notes |
|---|---|---|---|---|---|---|---|---|---|---|---|
| 1564 | 55588 | 3 | 1874 | 8/24 | 1 | 1571 | 55842 | 209 | Reb. | Both | Close- |
| 1564 | 55649 | 112 | 1875 | 8/24 | 2 | | + 55848 | + 232 | 1924 | 4/31 | Coupled |
| 1564 | 55679 | 149 | 1879 | 8/24 | 2 | 1572 | 55850 | 65 | 1908 | 6/43 | 7 |
| 1564 | 55704 | 179 | 1881 | 8/24 | To 381s | 1573 | 55863 | 326 | 1907 | 1927 | See Text |
| 1565 | 55723 | 143 | 1878 | 8/24 | 1 | 1574 | 55870 | 354 | 1916 | 9/50 | |
| 1566 | 55728 | 28 | 1894 | 1/35 | 3 | 1574 | 55873 | 357 | 1916 | BR | |
| 1567 | 55732 | 85 | 1890 | 10/27 | To 386s | 1575 | 55879 | 274 | 1900 | 5/44 | |
| 1567 | 55741 | 216 | 1888 | 9/27 | | 1575 | 55896 | 310 | 1902 | 6/43 | |
| 1568 | 55763 | 79 | 1895 | 3/47 | | 1576 | 55897 | 25 | 1922 | BR | |
| 1568 | 55764 | 80 | 1895 | 10/38 | 4 | 1576 | 55907 | 373 | 1922 | 1971 | See Text |
| 1568 | 55781 | 234 | 1896 | 5/47 | 5 | 1576 | 55911 | 377 | 1922 | BR | |
| 1568 | 55792 | 245 | 1898 | 3/39 | 6 | 1577 | 55934 | 339 | 1916 | 7/48 | |
| 1568 | 55815 | 285 | 1900 | 5/38 | | 1577 | 55942 | 347 | 1916 | BR | |
| 1568 | 55840 | 324 | 1906 | 5/35 | To 905s | 1757 | 62825 | 198 | 1882 | 9/27 | ED 8 |
| 1569 | 55843 | 210 | 1888 | 10/27 | To 385s | 1760 | 62849 | | Reb. 4/37 | BR | ED |
| 1570 | 55609 | 32 | Reb. | Both | Close- | 1760 | 62855 | | Reb. 12/37 | BR | 'ED |
| | + 55650 | + 113 | 3/24 | 1/26 | Coupled | | | | | | |

Notes:
1. SR number not carried
2. Both vans possibly close-coupled during 1923/4
3. Allocated to work between Ashford and Hythe only, 11/32
4. Allocated to Rye, for Harbour branch only, circa 1937
5. Allocated to work between Havant and Hayling Island only, 10/32
6. Allocated to Northfleet, for local trips only, circa 1937
7. To departmental van No. 906s from 5/35 to 9/38
8. This Stroudley van was built by the Midland RC&W Co., part of an 1882 order for 24 vehicles, LBSCR Nos. 181-204

# Chapter 7
## Bolster and Timber Wagons

These were the second largest group of wagons on the LBSCR, at the Grouping totalling nearly 650 vehicles or 6 per cent of the goods fleet. This gives some idea of how important the carriage of timber once was in Southern England. There were basically only three types of bolster wagon but each appeared in two capacities. The Southern Railway, therefore, allocated a total of six diagrams, whereas the LBSCR contented itself with just three. Many wagons were uprated in capacity both before and after the Grouping. Twenty of the single bolsters were sent to the Isle of Wight from 1928-30 and remained in service until very recently. Needless to say, these were the final survivors and outlived their mainland counterparts by over 30 years. Details of the SR diagrams are as follows:

| SR Diagram | LBSCR Diagram | Capacity (Tons) | Vehicle Type | Length Over Headstocks | Wheel-base | Known Construction Period | Remarks |
|---|---|---|---|---|---|---|---|
| 1616 | 16 | 6 | Single Bolster | 12ft. 0in. | 7ft. 0in. | 1880-1911* | 15 to IOW from 1928-30 |
| 1619 | 16 | 10 | Single Bolster | 12ft. 0in. | 7ft. 0in. | 1909 | |
| 1617 | 17 | 6 | Single Bolster | 13ft. 0in. | 6ft. 9in. | 1912-1914 | 5 to IOW in 1928 |
| 1620 | 17 | 10 | Single Bolster | 13ft. 0in. | 6ft. 9in. | 1922 | |
| 1618 | 18 | 8 | Double Bolster | 23ft. 0in. | 10ft. 6in. | 1891-1903 | |
| 1621 | 18 | 10 | Double Bolster | 23ft. 0in. | 10ft. 6in. | 1891-1901 | |
| – | – | 20 | Triple Bolster (six-wheeled) | 29ft. 11in. | 9ft. 9in. + 9ft. 9in. | 1909 | See Text |

\* Most survivors at the Grouping date from 1902 onwards

The six-wheeled triple bolster wagons were constructed on old coach underframes, and appear to have been something of an experiment. Only two were completed and neither survived to become Southern Railway stock, their LBSCR numbers being reallocated to aeroplane wagons in 1917. Luckily an official photograph recorded these vehicles for posterity and is reproduced as **Plate 94** on **page 52**.

**Plate 86** Short single bolster No. 59039, photographed on the Isle of Wight in 1948. Fifteen of these, plus five of the larger single bolsters went to the Island from 1928-30 and were renumbered on transfer. The former mainland numbers of this wagon were SR 58458 and LBSCR 7486. It dates from 1911. All Isle of Wight examples were uprated to 10 tons capacity, as were most of the later survivors on the mainland.

*A. E. West*

**Figure 22** This is a drawing of both types of single bolster wagons, showing typical lettering styles.

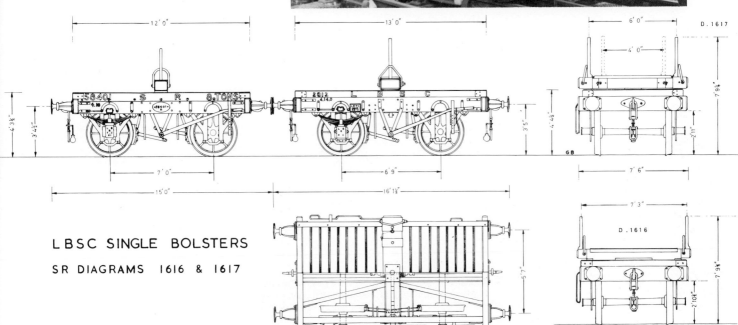

## LBSC SINGLE BOLSTERS
### SR DIAGRAMS 1616 & 1617

**Plate 87** A very typical load for two single bolster wagons. In this case they are carrying heavy timbers, destined for reconstruction work on Ryde Pier. Nos. DS59040 and 59051 are allocated to the Engineers and sport a typical 1960s lettering style. Their former mainland numbers were, respectively, SR 58412 and 58384, originally LBSCR 7251 and 7206. Both were completed in 1909, probably with double block brakes. By the time of transfer to the Isle of Wight, they had Freighter brake gear.

*A. Blackburn*

**Plate 88** One of the larger single bolster wagons to Diagram 1617/20 at Newport (Monmouth) in 1926. It was not renumbered until February 1930. LBSCR No. 2866 dates from 1912 and was uprated from 6 to 10 tons in November 1923. SR number 58504 was allocated and the vehicle remained in traffic until July 1946, being one of the last surviving mainland examples. Freighter brake gear was provided on all Diagram 1617/20 single bolsters. The original cost of this wagon was a mere £51 and we may safely assume that both the LBSCR and the SR obtained good value for their money!

*Authors' Collection*

**Plate 89** Another single bolster wagon to SR Diagram 1620. This type of wagon normally ran in sets; the vehicles themselves did not have to be of the same diagram, although they very often were, any discrepancy in bolster height being made good by packings. On this occasion, LBSCR No. 7913 was probably being used as a runner to the wagon on the right. Note the screw couplings and the binding chains with which this class of wagon was always provided. No. 7913 was withdrawn in April 1929 without having been repainted in SR livery or being renumbered; its intended SR number was 58636. The photograph was taken two years earlier, at Crystal Palace.

*E. R. Lacey*

**Plate 90** LBSCR batten wagons, or double bolster wagons as they have more recently been called, look decidedly ancient, possibly on account of their rather short wheelbase. Most wagons of this type have a wheelbase (and bolster spacing) of about 12ft. LBSCR No. 7726 (later SR No. 58876) dates from 1900, and was officially photographed in 1907. Uprated from 8 to 10 tons in 1922, it was allocated to SR Diagram 1621. Withdrawal came in 1930. Note the single block brakes. Most LBSCR wagons built after 1894 had double block brakes.

*British Rail*

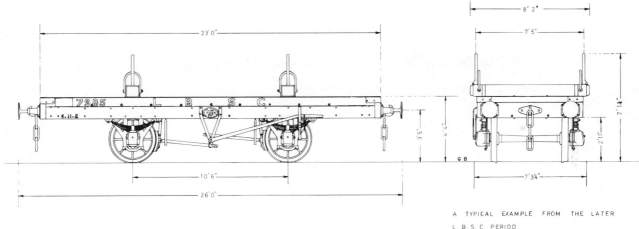

## LBSC DOUBLE BOLSTER
### SR DIAGRAM 1618

A TYPICAL EXAMPLE FROM THE LATER
L.B.S.C PERIOD

**Figure 23** This illustrates a more modern example.

**Plate 91** This interesting picture illustrates SR No. 58836 at King's Cross Shed on 14th September 1935. The press photographer was officially recording LNER A4 Pacific *Silver Link* and has clearly found a good use for this double bolster wagon to Diagram 1621. The wagon is loaded with a gas holder. Its former LBSCR number was 4042 and attention is drawn to the lower plate on page 63 of *LB&SCR Album* by K. Marx and J. Minnis, which features LBSCR bolster No. 4042. They are presumably the same vehicle, despite the fact that they have different axleboxes and brakes. Built in 1893, it was uprated from 8 to 10 tons in June 1923, receiving oil axleboxes and Freighter brakes at the same time. Withdrawal did not take place until October 1943.

*H. F. Wheeller*

**Plate 92** Few LBSCR bolster wagons entered departmental use, although four double bolster wagons were appropriated for special duties and were renumbered as SR 61066-9 in 1930. This shows No. 236S at Ashford Works in 1951, having lost its bolsters. Converted for service use in March 1945, the former numbers were SR 58783 and LBSCR 10508. It was built in 1901 with double block brakes but later received Freighter gear.

*A. E. West*

**Plate 93** Several double bolster wagons were modified as crane runners, No. DS3135 being a typical example, seen at Bude in September 1961. This has received new side and end planks as well as a coat of BR light grey paint. Built in 1898 as LBSCR No. 7548, it became SR No. 58855 and finally departmental 3135s in 1945. Again, double block brakes were originally provided, these being altered to the Freighter type in SR days.

*A. E. West*

**Plate 94** A 20 ton triple bolster wagon, No. 7281, as outshopped in November 1909. Built for carrying heavy timbers and rails, these were splendid looking wagons and it is a great pity that they failed to become SR property, at least not in the form illustrated. According to LBSCR records both wagons were reconstructed as aeroplane trucks in 1917, retaining the same running numbers. As such, they became SR Diagram 1689, and are described in the next chapter. **Plate 102** illustrates wagon No. 7281 as it appeared after rebuilding. Comparison of the two vehicles reveals many extensive alterations, and the authors are not convinced that much, if any, of the triple bolster wagons were actually incorporated into the rebuilds. The 1910 LBSCR diagram of the triple bolster wagon states that the vehicles could not negotiate curves of less than 5 chains radius.

*British Rail*

### Examples of numbering (for full SR details refer to Appendix 1)

| SR Diagram | SR Number | LBSCR Number | Date Built | With-drawn | Brake Gear | SR Diagram | SR Number | LBSCR Number | Date Built | With-drawn | Brake Gear |
|---|---|---|---|---|---|---|---|---|---|---|---|
| 1616 | 58445 | 7323 | 6/11 | 4/50 | DB, F 7/29 | 1619 | 58785 | 7238 | 6/09 | 5/31 | DB |
| 1616 | 58466 | 7549 | 6/11 | 3/45 | DB, F 6/28 | 1620 | 58813 | 4582 | 6/22 | 12/49 | F |
| 1617 | 58471 | 2805 | 12/12 | 4/49 | F | 1620 | 58825 | 7534 | 6/22 | 1/49 | F |
| 1617 | 58530 | 2910 | 12/12 | 7/50 | F | 1621 | 58886 | 7994 | 1895 | 1/49 | SB, later F |
| 1618* | 58668 | 4526 | 1903 | 8/33 | Prob. DB | 1621 | 58910 | 10507 | 1901 | 11/30 | Prob. DB |
| 1618 | 58752 | 7987 | 1895 | 12/47 | SB, later F | Triple Bolster | | 7282 | 1909 | 1917 | ES |

\* By 1923 this wagon carried just one centrally-placed bolster

# Chapter 8
## Road Vehicle Trucks, Machinery Trucks and Special Wagons

Unlike most pre-Grouping companies, the LBSCR described its road vehicle trucks as machinery wagons and labelled them accordingly. The authors have therefore decided to include these along with the special wagons, most of which were also suitable for the conveyance of machinery. Road vehicle trucks apart, LBSCR special wagons were an extremely rare breed, comprising just twenty vehicles of about eight different types. It may be assumed that they were rarely seen in the average goods yard or train, probably being based at one or more of the larger yards (e.g. New Cross, Norwood, Battersea or Brighton), and released to traffic as required. Certainly the lack of photographs of them in service bears out this theory.

The various Southern Railway diagrams are summarised below.

| SR Diagram | LBSCR Diagram | Capacity (Tons) | Vehicle Type | Length Over Headstocks | Wheel-base | Known Construction Period | Remarks |
|---|---|---|---|---|---|---|---|
| 1661 | 19 | 10 | Road Vehicle/ Machinery Truck | 16ft. 6in. | 10ft. 5in. | 1892-1923 | 19 to IOW in 1928/9 |
| 1684 | 15 | 6 | Plate Glass Wagon | 26ft. 0in. | 17ft. 0in. | 1898 | |
| 1685 | 28 | 12 | Bogie Aeroplane Truck | 38ft. 0in. | Bogie Ccs. 26ft. 0in. | Reb. 6/23 | Underframe ex-bogie van |
| 1686 | 20 | 20 | Machinery/Well Wagon | 20ft. 2in. | 15ft. 0in. | 1893 | SR Code 'Well D' |
| 1687 | 30 | 20 | Bogie Aeroplane Truck | 48ft. 0in. | Bogie Ccs. 36ft. 0in. | 1904 | Ex-Timber trucks, 1915 |
| 1688 | 31 | 30 | 8w Machinery Wagon/Boiler Truck | 35ft. 0in. | 5ft. + 10ft. + 5ft. | 1889 | Based at Brighton |
| 1689 | 32 | 4 | Aeroplane Truck | 29ft. 11in. | 20ft. 0in. | Reb. 1917 | Ex-bolster |
| | - | 4 | Aeroplane Truck | 29ft. 11in. | 19ft. 6in. | Reb. 8/25 | Ex-ballast |
| 1705 | 26 | 7 | Gunpowder Van | 18ft. 4in. | 9ft. 9in. | 1903-1904 | |

Some reclassification of the aeroplane trucks took place between 1923 and 1925. The two original vehicles to Diagram 1689 were classified by the Southern Railway as points and crossings wagons, being allocated Diagram 1752. This diagram appears never to have been issued, and the vehicles were reallocated SR Diagram 1689 in July 1923. The six-wheeled ballast wagon was allocated SR Diagram 1756 in its original form, but was reconstructed as an aeroplane truck in August 1925, apparently also to Diagram 1689, but this is not made clear in the SR registers. It is uncertain whether the vehicle remained a six wheeler or was reduced to four wheels.

**Plate 95** The 1882 series of pictures include road vehicle/machinery truck No. 7067. Points to note are the old style grease axleboxes and wooden pads on the buffers, typical of the late Craven and early Stroudley era. The livery is somewhat unclear, but the 'illiterate' symbol, Company initials and code 'Machinery' are just visible.
*British Rail*

**Plate 96** Despite their code name 'Machinery', these wagons were also employed for carrying containers. This is illustrated by LBSCR Nos. 7005 (SR No. 60427), 7160, 7081 and 7095 at Eastbourne, circa 1906. The ex-LCDR road vehicle truck is stencilled 'For Highway Vehicles'. Apart from LBSCR No. 7005 and SECR No. 11952, none of the other wagons visible became SR property. These two wagons have double block brakes, and the remainder have single block. Only wagon No. 7005, has oil axleboxes. Curtiss & Sons Ltd. were a Portsmouth-based firm specialising in the removal business.
*Authors' Collection*

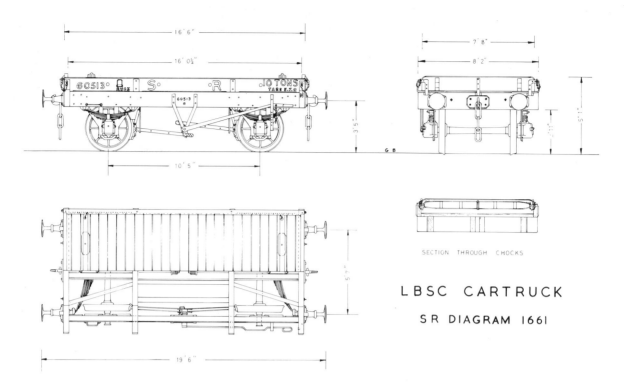

**LBSC CARTRUCK**

**SR DIAGRAM 1661**

SECTION THROUGH CHOCKS

**Figure 24**  This illustrates a typical vehicle to SR Diagram 1661.

**Plate 97**  The final style of LBSCR lettering is carried by machinery truck No.7577, photographed at Worthing between 1923 and 1929. This vehicle was one of fifteen completed shortly after the Grouping, but was outshopped in LBSCR livery. Renumbering as SR 60542 took place at New Cross Gate on 13th November 1929. Note the non common user 'N' code letter on the headstock ends. Four-hole disc wheels and Freighter brakes were provided and the wagon ran until 1948. The original cost was £211.

*E. R. Lacey*

**Plate 98**  The nineteen wagons transferred to the Isle of Wight were, not surprisingly, the last in service, several running until 1966. In contrast, the last mainland example was condemned in November 1950. Two island transfers are seen below, photographed at Ryde St. John's in April 1936, together with an ex-SECR dropside wagon. Notice the minor variations in lettering layout and the SR code name 'RUCK'. Details of the LBSCR wagons are:

| SR IOW No. | SR Mainland No. | LBSCR No. | Date Built | Date to IOW | Withdrawn |
|---|---|---|---|---|---|
| 60569 | 60520 | 7112 | 1892 | 8/28 | 4/37 |
| 60579 | 60536 | 7129 | 1923 | 7/29 | 1966 |

No. 60579 is now owned by the Wight Locomotive Society at Havenstreet.

*S. W. Baker*

Plate 99 By 1948, ex-LBSCR machinery trucks were a rare sight on the mainland, and therefore this wagon is of considerable interest. It shows No. S60515 at Feltham in March 1950, bearing an early British Railways style of lettering and an overhaul date of December 1949. Note the BR code 'Cartruck'. Built in 1912 as LBSCR No. 7099, its original cost is recorded as a mere £50. This is remarkably low and may indicate the use of second-hand parts.

*A. E. West*

**Examples of numbering (see Appendix 1 for full details)**

| SR Number | LBSCR Number | Built | Withdrawn | Brake Gear |
| --- | --- | --- | --- | --- |
| 60451 | 7029 | 12/10 | 11/50 | DB, F 1928. |
| 60456 | 7036 | 12/12 | 12/46 | F |
| 60519 | 7111 | 1892 | 9/27 | SB |
| 60541 | 7572 | 12/23 | 5/49 | F |

**Figure 25** A drawing of the 20 ton well/machinery wagon, six examples of which were built in 1893.

## L B S C  W E L L  W A G O N   S R  D I A G R A M  1 6 8 6

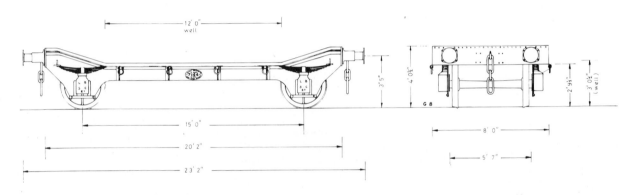

DRAWING  BASED  PARTLY  ON  PHOTOGRAPHS

We shall now consider those vehicles which were truly special wagons. The four-wheeled well wagon was also suitable for carrying machinery and is described as such on some LBSCR diagrams. LBSCR numbers were 7141-6, later SR Nos. 61073-8. All six survived at the Grouping but only Nos. 7141-4 received their allocated SR numbers. By 1930, No. 7143 had been withdrawn, leaving only three in service. Of these, SR No. 61073 was easily the last in traffic,

receiving either-side brakes in June 1933, being uprated to 21 tons in June 1943, and was finally condemned in May 1946. The only photographs known to the authors all depict wagon No. 7144 which was adapted in 1894 to carry a 40 pounder Armstrong gun, for use by the 1st Sussex Artillery Volunteers, and was part of a complete armoured train built by the LBSCR at Brighton Works.

**Plate 100** This illustrates the well wagon, photographed in the paint shop at Brighton. The actual train was given considerable press coverage at the time, but then faded into obscurity. Its last recorded use was in 1900, after which wagon No. 7144 returned to more mundane duties. Regrettably no information regarding the normal duties of these vehicles are known. Note the complete absence of brake gear on the vehicles when built.

*Authors' Collection*

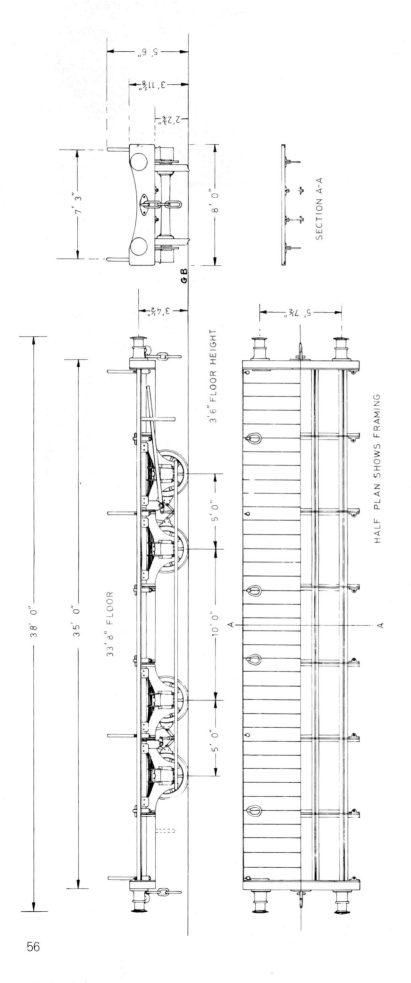

5' 6"

3' 11⅝"

2' 2¾"

7' 3"

8' 0"

GB

SECTION A-A

3' 4½"

3' 6" FLOOR HEIGHT

38' 0"

35' 0"

33' 8" FLOOR

5' 0"

10' 0"

5' 0"

A

5' 7½"

HALF PLAN SHOWS FRAMING

A

# LBSC 30 TON MACHINERY WAGON

## SR DIAGRAM 1688

Probably the most unusual wagon taken over by the Southern Railway at the Grouping was this 30 ton machinery wagon. It was a rigid eight-wheeled vehicle and, almost certainly, spent most of its life in and around the area of Brighton Works, transporting boilers and other similar heavy equipment. Numbered 7107 in LBSCR stock, it was subject to certain specific operating restrictions. The August 1922 Appendix to the service timetable states the following: 'Trucks of exceptional construction (20 ton bogie trucks 10552-10554, 30 ton machinery truck 7107 and Engineers 20 ton bogie rail trucks). These trucks must not be loaded with anything to project over either end, to

necessitate a Guard (i.e. match) Truck. When loaded they must be marshalled in Goods Trains between loaded trucks. If there are no loaded trucks in the train, they must be marshalled either next behind the engine or next in front of the rear Brake.'

The wagon dates from 1889 and was allocated SR number 61082 at the Grouping. This number was never carried, as the wagon was transferred to the duplicate service stock list as No. 01159s in 1926, for use between Preston Park and Brighton Works. It was withdrawn in February 1930.

**Figure 26**
Lettering details are not known

**Figure 27**

3' 11½"
3' 0"
8' 0"

BODY AND SOLEBARS 8' 0" WIDE.
FOUR TRUSS RODS PLACED AT 10⅜"
AND 3' 7⅜" EITHER SIDE OF CENTRE.

GB

41' 0"
3' 4½"
5' 6"
20' 6"
5' 6"
5' 7"
38' 0"

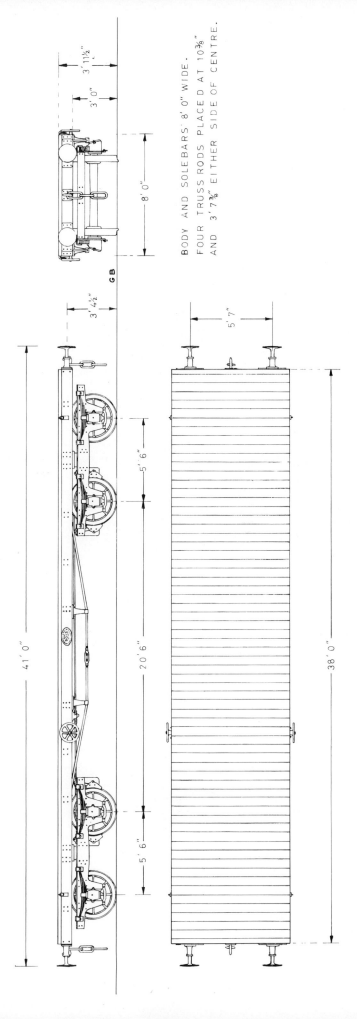

# LBSC FLAT WAGON EX. REFRIGERATOR VAN   SR. DIAGRAM No 1685

### Aeroplane Trucks

These were, basically, flat wagons which could carry any bulky (and usually) light load. Three bogie vehicles were converted from 25 ton bogie timber wagons in 1915, one more was converted from the bogie refrigerator van underframe in 1923 (**see Figure 27 above**), and there were also two four wheelers. One more was converted in 1925. None survived for long under SR ownership. Details are as below.

| SR Diagram | SR Numbers | LBSCR Numbers | With-drawn | Notes |
|---|---|---|---|---|
| 1685 | 61072 | 9013 | 2/29 | Underframe ex-bogie refrigerator van in June 1923 |
| 1687 | 61079 | 10552 | 2/29 | Downrated to 12 tons, post-1923 |
| 1687 | 61080 | 10553 | 11/28 | Downrated to 12 tons, post-1923 |
| 1687 | 61081 | 10554 | 8/24 | SR number not carried |
| 1689 | 61083 | 7281 | 4/34 | Originally allocated SR numbers 62607/8 to Diagram 1752 |
| 1689 | 61084 | 7282* |  |  |
| 1689 | 61085 | 8432* | 5/33 | Ex-Diagram 1756 in August 1925 |

*Number carried as six-wheeled ballast wagon.

**Plate 101** The only photograph of a bogie aeroplane truck known to the authors, this shows LBSCR No. 10553 at East Croydon in 1919, loaded with two captured German artillery guns. The conversion appears to have simply involved the removal of bolsters and the addition of rope hooks.

*Authors' Collection*

**Plate 102** Four-wheeled aeroplane truck No. 7281 at Lancing Works in April 1917. This, according to LBSCR records, is the same vehicle that features in **Plate 94**. However, the modifications are considerable and include altering the wheelbase from 19ft. 6in. to 20ft. 0in. Possibly only such fittings as buffers, wheel sets and axleboxes were incorporated into the rebuilds.

*T. A. Barry Collection*

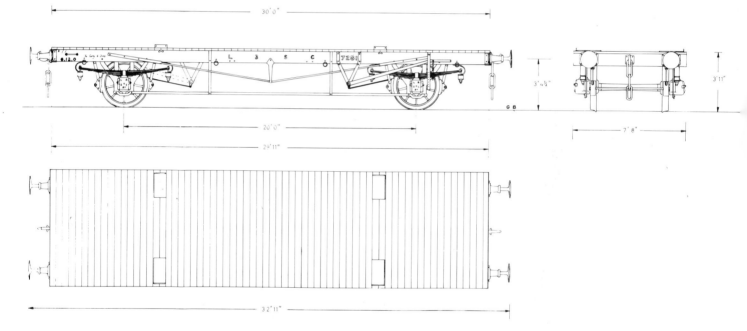

## LBSC 4 TON AEROPLANE WAGON
### SR DIAGRAM 1689

**Figure 28** This illustrates the wagons in their original state. Neither received its SR number until 1928.

The third example of Diagram 1689 is something of a mystery vehicle. This was allocated SR number 62822 at the Grouping, being a 20 ton, six-wheeled, ballast wagon. This number appears not to have been carried, and reconstruction to an aeroplane truck took place in August 1925. The exact manner in which the conversion was accomplished is not recorded, and the authors are unable to state whether it resembled **Figure 28** or not. The vehicle may have retained six wheels, but no separate diagram has so far come to light.

Four double bolster wagons were reclassified as special wagons in 1930, being allocated SR numbers 61066-9. It is not known for what purpose they were used, nor if they were modified in any way. It is possible that they were stripped of bolsters and used for aeroplane traffic, but no new Southern Railway diagram was issued to cover any such modification.

With the rapid development of aeroplane technology in the 1920s and early 1930s, the requirement for aeroplane trucks rapidly diminished, the size of components soon becoming too large to be readily carried by rail. Consequently, this class of wagon disappeared from railway parlance in the 1930s. Although not confined to the carriage of aeroplane parts, the fact that they were always regarded as special wagons by the Southern Railway may have limited their use. It would seem that of the other 'Big Four' companies, only the GWR classed aeroplane trucks as special vehicles. In contrast, the SECR and LSWR went in for aeroplane vans, but these were classified as passenger stock.

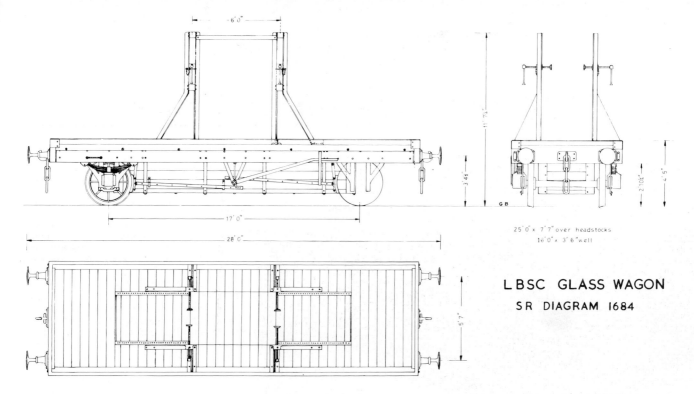

**LBSC GLASS WAGON**
**SR DIAGRAM 1684**

**Figure 29** This shows the LBSCR plate glass wagon. There were only two such vehicles, LBSCR Nos. 5374/5, later allocated SR numbers 61070/1. Both were built in 1898, and were withdrawn in July 1933 and October 1930 respectively. No photographs are known to the authors, and no information is available regarding their duties or where they were based. The only known sighting was in March 1927, when an observer at Eastleigh saw LBSCR No. 5374, still in pre-Grouping livery, pass through in the direction of Southampton, in company with one of the bogie aeroplane trucks. Both wagons received SR livery, being renumbered in June 1928 (No. 61070) and November 1929 (No. 61071). In appearance, the wagons closely resemble the LSWR design. It should be remembered that A. H. Panter was appointed to the LBSCR in 1898.

**L B S C  GUNPOWDER VAN**  SR DIAGRAM 1705

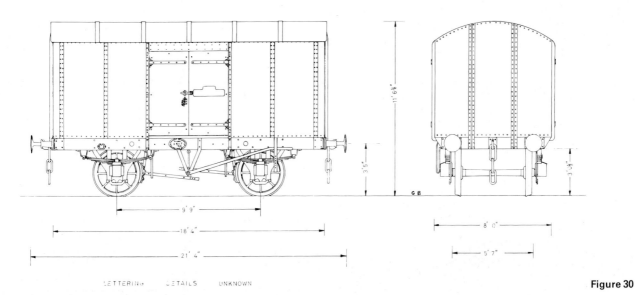

**Figure 30**

The four gunpowder vans were allocated SR numbers 61261-4, formerly LBSCR numbers 1517/41 (built in 1903) and 9029/30 (built in 1904). They were based at New Cross in pre-Grouping days. According to both LBSCR and SR diagrams, the vans were a steel-clad version of the standard LBSCR covered goods wagon. However, two general arrangement drawings survive; one showing a timber-planked vehicle, the other a steel version. In the absence of any photographic confirmation, the authors are of the opinion that the latter design was built. The tare weight of 9 tons 19cwt. also points to a steel vehicle. SR No. 61261 was scrapped in 1929, but the others lasted much longer. The final survivor was No. 61263, withdrawn in 1948. Freighter brakes were provided in May 1930.

59

# Chapter 9
# Engineer's Department Wagons

As usual, the Southern Railway divided these into two groups; ballast wagons/brake vans and rail/sleeper wagons. Before the Grouping, the administration of the Engineer's Department was split into two sections — the Northern Division based at Fairfield Yard (East Croydon) and covering the London area, the Southern Division based at Brighton and covering the remainder of the Company's permanent way. Many wagons were allocated to one or other division and were lettered ND or SD, as appropriate. In Southern Railway days, other permanent way depots were set up, the best known being at New Cross Gate and Three Bridges.

**Plate 103** For some reason photographs of LBSCR ballast trains are fairly common. Here we see E3 class radial tank No. 165 heading an 'up' Southern Division ballast train into Dorking, probably just before the Grouping. Both brake vans are Stroudley vehicles to SR Diagram 1564. Neither are actually stencilled 'Ballast' so were not permanently allocated to the Engineer's Department. The leading van, No. 22, dates from 1887, and was withdrawn in October 1924 before receiving its allocated SR number, 55604. All the other vehicles are to Diagram 1754.

*Authors' Collection*

## Ballast Wagons and Brake Vans

These are summarised as follows:

| SR Diagram | LBSCR Diagram | Capacity (Tons) | Vehicle Type | Length Over Headstocks | Wheel-base | Known Construction Period | Remarks |
|---|---|---|---|---|---|---|---|
| 1751 | 37 | 4 | Two Plank Dropside Ballast | 12ft. 0in. | 7ft. 0in. | 1866-1891 | Dumb buffers 18 to IOW, 1927 |
| 1752 | 32 | 4 | Points and Crossings Wagon | 29ft. 11in. | 20ft. 0in. | Reb. 1917 | To Diagram 1689, 7/23 |
| 1753 | 38 | 6 | Three Plank Dropside Ballast | 12ft. 0in. | 7ft. 0in. | 1896-1905 | Dumb buffers |
| 1754 | 39 | 15 | Three Plank Dropside Ballast | 20ft. 0in. | 12ft. 0in. | 1905-1921 | Some ex-BRCW Some details to RCH Specification |
| 1755 | 40 | 20 | Ballast Hopper | 20ft. 0in. | 12ft. 0in. | 1903-1904 | 10 to IOW, 1947 |
| 1756 | 49 | 20 | 6w Three Plank Dropside Ballast | 29ft. 11in. | 9ft. 9in. + 9ft. 9in. | 1910 | To Diagram 1689, 8/25 |
| 1757 | 21 | 8 | Ballast Brake Van | 16ft. 0in. | 9ft. 9in. | 1872-1889 | **See Chapter 6** |
| 1758 | 46 | 8 | Ballast Brake Van | 20ft. 0in. | 11ft. 6in. | 1896/1901 | |
| 1759 | 47 | 20 | 6w Ballast Brake Van | 20ft. 0in. | 5ft. 9in. + 5ft. 9in. | 1915-1916 | |
| 1760 | — | 20 | Ballast Brake Van | 24ft. 0in. | 16ft. 0in. | Reb. 1928/9 & 1937 | ex-Diagram 1576. **See Chapter 6** |

The unique six-wheeled ballast wagon was an experimental vehicle constructed on a spare carriage underframe. In detail it resembled the 15 ton vehicles to Diagram 1754, having three sets of drop doors on each side. It was reclassified and rebuilt as an aeroplane truck in 1925.

**Plate 104** Typical of the many archaic LBSCR ballast wagons is this two plank dumb-buffered example, photographed in 1882. This vehicle failed to survive at the Grouping but, surprisingly, 75 wagons of this type were still in stock in 1923 and over half of these actually received their allocated Southern Railway numbers. SR Diagram 1751 was issued. The 'illiterate' symbol is just visible over the LBSCR number, 7796. Notice the timber brake block and the canvas flaps over the axleboxes; these were intended to protect the bearings from the effects of stone dust. In 1896, the LBSCR purchased ninety second-hand wagons from Birmingham Railway, Carriage & Wagon Company, allocating them numbers 8411-8500. At least two were of this type, the rest being to Diagram 1753 but dimensionally were very similar.

*British Rail*

Lancing Railway Station.

**Plate 105** A view of Lancing Station looking east, circa 1910. The ballast train comprises a radial tank, Stroudley brake van, 'B' class open and two plank dropside wagons to Diagram 1751. Note the rather unusual end profile of some of the vehicles. There were others with an end profile similar to the 'D' class open goods wagons.

*Lens of Sutton*

**Plate 106 (Right)** A few wagons entered SR departmental service, such as No. 01127S, photographed at Newhaven in September 1931. Eighteen of these vehicles were transferred to the Isle of Wight in 1927 and used on the Brading to Sandown widening works. The last Isle of Wight example was scrapped in April 1931, and some remained in LBSCR livery to the end.

*L. E. Brailsford*

**Plate 107 (Right)** The three plank dropside wagons were very similar and over seventy survived at the Grouping. All except six received SR livery of red oxide with white lettering, Diagram 1753 being allocated. No. 62634 was photographed at Hoo Junction (SECR) in September 1931. It was built in 1900 for the sum of £30, the former LBSCR number being 7801. Withdrawal took place in April 1932.

*R. W. Kidner*

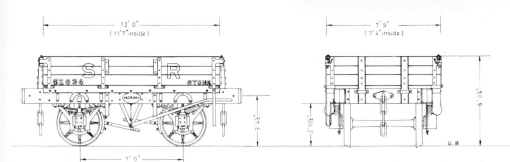

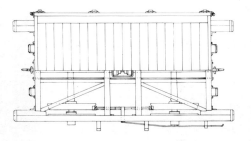

## LBSC 6 TON BALLAST
### SR DIAGRAM 1753

THERE WAS A SIMILAR 2 PLANK 4 TON VERSION.
SEE DIAGRAM 1755 FOR A DESIGN PRODUCED
ONLY 5 YEARS LATER

**Figure 31** This is a drawing of the three plank dropside wagon. Most of these were equipped with double block brakes, and the two plank wagons had single block gear. Withdrawal of both types was completed in 1933, several of the final survivors being used at Southampton during the construction of the New Docks. By this time they were amongst the last railway-owned wagons with dumb buffers in this country.

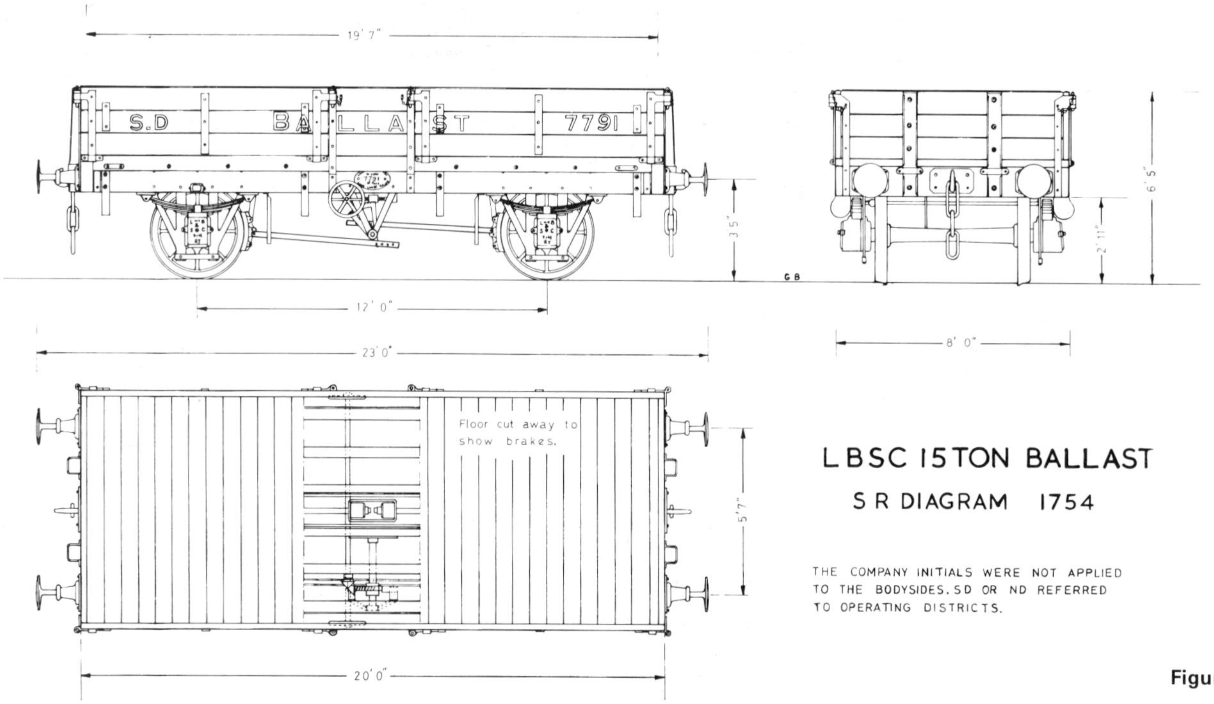

**L B S C 15 TON BALLAST**

**S R DIAGRAM 1754**

THE COMPANY INITIALS WERE NOT APPLIED
TO THE BODYSIDES. SD OR ND REFERRED
TO OPERATING DISTRICTS.

**Figure 32**

**Plate 108**  The final dumb-buffered wagons appeared in 1905, and it is rather remarkable that the next LBSCR design was so modern. This view depicts 15 ton dropside wagon No. 8496 when new in 1914, allocated to the Northern Division. These vehicles became the standard LBSCR ballast wagons from 1905 until the Grouping, 112 examples being allocated SR Diagram 1754. LBSCR No. 8496 subsequently became SR No. 62787, running until December 1947. These wagons were unusual in that they employed RCH standard journal spacing, the first use of such details by the LBSCR. This probably explains why several lasted until the 1960s.

*British Rail*

**Plate 109**  SR No. 62708 at Stewarts Lane in 1935. Built in 1906 as LBSCR No. 8413, it ran until June 1937. Note the steel door stops on this vehicle compared with the timber ones on No. 8496. Although only two brake blocks are provided, the screw gear allows the brake to be applied from either side of the vehicle.

*G. Y. Hemingway*

Many of these wagons were ordered as replacements for the dumb-buffered stock and were numbered between 8411 and 8500.

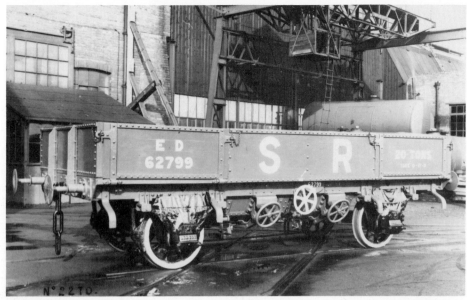

**Plate 110** Just prior to the construction of the 15 ton ballast wagons, the Company took delivery of thirty steel ballast hopper wagons from Messrs Hurst, Nelson & Co. of Motherwell (see **Frontispiece** for a photograph of one of these unusual wagons in its original condition). LBSCR numbers were 10510-39, (later SR Nos. 62792-62821). Purchased at a cost of £174 each, they were allocated SR Diagram 1755. All thirty were modified by Chas. Roberts & Co. in 1930, the unloading mechanism being rebuilt. In this form we see SR No. 62799 as lettered by the contractor.

*Authors' Collection*

**Plate 111** Ten of these wagons were transferred to the Isle of Wight circa 1947, but were not renumbered or repainted. SR No. 62810 was photographed soon after, still with an 'Empty to Eastleigh Ballast Sdg' instruction on the side. Note that the 1930 lettering 'SR' is still visible; some wagons retained traces of these initials in the early 1960s! The last Isle of Wight example was scrapped in 1955, but those on the mainland lasted until 1959-61. All were uprated from 20 to 21 tons in 1939.

*F. Foote*

# LBSC 20 TON BALLAST HOPPER SR DIAGRAM 1755

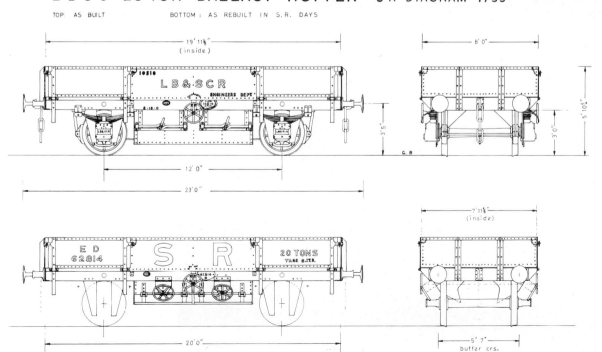

**Figure 33** This illustrates the wagons in both original and rebuilt state.

**Plate 112** An interesting comparison between four and six-wheeled ballast brake vans in SR pre-1936 livery. Although superficially alike, modellers should note that the four wheelers had doors directly opposite each other, and the six wheelers had them in diagonally opposite corners. Van No. 62831 dates from 1901, its LBSCR number being 233. No. 62837 dates from 1916 and was formerly LBSCR No. 330. Respective costs were £95 and £332. The former was withdrawn in December 1943, and the latter exactly a decade later.

*E. Jackson*

## L B S C 7T.15 BALLAST BRAKE    SR DIAGRAM 1758

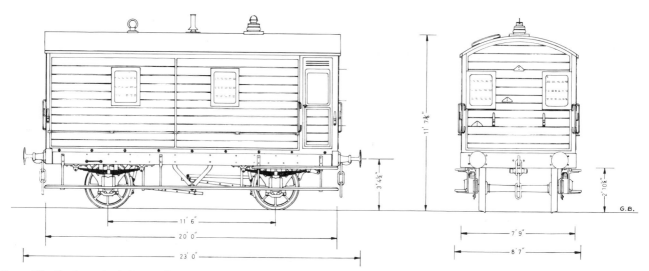

**Figure 34**    The four-wheeled van to SR Diagram 1758.

**Plate 113** An excellent picture of a Southern Railway ballast train, hauled by Class C2X 0-6-0 No. B440, circa 1928. The leading van is No. 62832 and this is followed by twelve ballast wagons to Diagram 1754. Next comes one of four LCDR coaches converted to ballast brake vans in 1927, followed by another LBSCR van to either Diagram 1758 or 1759. Another fifteen ballast wagons follow to Diagram 1754 with what appears to be a Stroudley brake van at the rear. The ballast wagons are liberally coated with chalk dust.

*Authors' Collection*

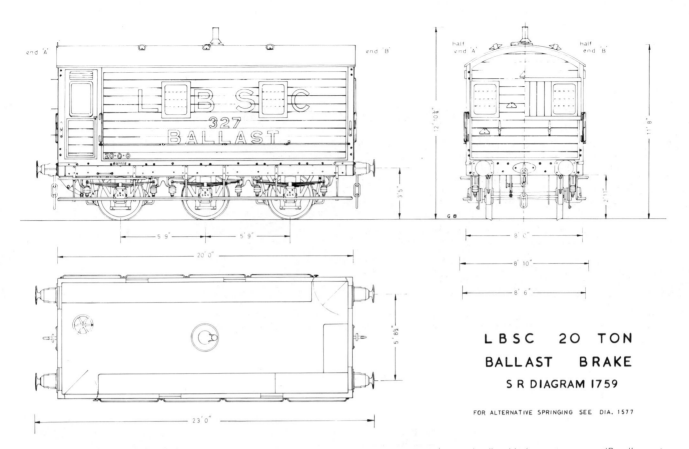

LBSC 20 TON
BALLAST BRAKE
SR DIAGRAM 1759

FOR ALTERNATIVE SPRINGING SEE DIA. 1577

**Figure 35** The six-wheeled van to SR Diagram 1759. These splendid-looking vehicles shared some details with the contemporary 'Road' vans to SR Diagram 1577, particularly with regard to underframe details.

**Plate 114** The official photograph of No. 327 as completed in October 1915 and finished in red livery. The subsequent Southern Railway number was 62834, and the vehicle ran until July 1947. Notice the sliding shutters which could be used to cover the end windows. One must pity the poor guard who expected to find one of these vans at the end of his train, but was instead given a Stroudley brake to Diagram 1757!

*British Rail*

**Plate 115** A three-quarter view of ballast brake No. 62837 in ex-works SR pre-1936 livery. The clean white roof would not have stayed in that condition for very long!

*E. Jackson*

Numbering details of these vehicles are:

| SR Dia. | LBSCR Numbers | SR Numbers |
|---|---|---|
| 1758 | 47, 73, 90-92, 233/93/4 | 62826-33 |
| 1759 | 327-332 | 62834-39 |

**Plate 116** A final view of Diagram 1759, SR No. 62835 at Three Bridges in September 1947, still showing faded pre-1936 livery. Compare this with the van in **Plate 114**. The sliding shutters have been removed from the end windows and lamp tops are visible in the roof, but otherwise the wagon is still in original condition. It was renumbered as S62835 in 1948 and scrapped in 1957.

*R. E. Tustin*

### Examples of numbering (for full SR details refer to Appendix 1)

| SR Diagram | SR Number | LBSCR Number | Date Built | With-drawn | Brake Gear | Notes |
|---|---|---|---|---|---|---|
| 1751 | 62553 | 7682 | 1878 | 12/33 | - | Brake gear details not recorded |
| 1751 | 62578 | 7836 | 1879 | 12/33 | - | Brake gear details not recorded |
| 1752 | 62608 | 7282 | 1917 | - | F | To aeroplane truck No. 61084 in July 1923 (see **Chapter 8** for full details) |
| 1753 | 62610 | 7574 | 1899 | 10/32 | - | Brake gear details not recorded |
| 1753 | 62631 | 7790 | 1900 | 12/31 | - | Brake gear details not recorded |
| 1754 | 62721 | 8426 | 1906 | 10/61 | SC | British Railways code name 'Ling' |
| 1754 | 62742 | 8449 | 1908 | 5/61 | SC | British Railways code name 'Ling' |
| 1755 | 62809 | 10527 | 1904 | 5/60 | SC | British Railways code name 'Ling' |
| 1755 | 62814 | 10532 | 1904 | 6/61 | SC | British Railways code name 'Ling' |
| 1756 | 62822 | 8432 | 1910 | - | SC | Rebuilt as aeroplane truck No. 61085 in August 1925 (see **Chapter 8** for full details) |
| 1758 | 62830 | 92 | 1896 | 5/38 | SC | |
| 1758 | 62833 | 294 | 1901 | 1/44 | SC | Last in service |
| 1759 | 62834 | 327 | 1915 | 7/47 | SC | |
| 1759 | 62835 | 328 | 1916 | 8/57 | SC | Last in service |

For details of SR Diagrams 1757 and 1760 see **Chapter 6**

### Rail and sleeper wagons

These are the final group of vehicles to appear in the Southern Railway capital stock numbering list. As usual with this class of wagon few photographs seem to have been taken. The SR diagrams are summarised below, together with one design which was transferred to departmental stock at the Grouping, and failed to receive a Southern Railway diagram number.

| SR Diagram | LBSCR Diagram | Capacity (Tons) | Vehicle Type | Length Over Headstocks | Wheelbase | Known Construction Period | Remarks |
|---|---|---|---|---|---|---|---|
| 1798 | 43 | 10 | Sleeper Wagon | 19ft. 0in. | 10ft. 6in. | 1891 | Similar to Batten Truck |
| 1799 | 41 | 12 | Ballast, Rail and Sleeper Wagon | 19ft. 0in. | 10ft. 6in. | 1897-1899 | Built by BRCW Co. |
| 1800 | 42 | 10 | Rail and Sleeper Wagon | 19ft. 0in. | 10ft. 6in. | 1894 | |
| 1801 | 42 | 12 | Rail and Sleeper Wagon | 19ft. 0in. | 10ft. 6in. | 1920-1921 | Built by Metropolitan |
| 1802 | 45 | 20* | Bogie Rail Wagon | 48ft. 0in. | Bogie Ccs 36ft. 0in. | 1904 | Built by Hurst, Nelson |
| 1803 | 21 | | Bogie Rail Wagon For Long Welded Rails | 48ft. 0in. | Bogie Ccs 36ft. 0in. | Reb. 1952 | Ex-Diagram 1802 Vac. piped |
| | 44 | 12 | Points and Crossing Wagon | 31ft. 2in. | 18ft. 0in. | 1901 | To service stock in 1923 |

* The bogie rail wagons were rated at 30 ton capacity when built, but were downrated to 20 tons in 1915. Three similar wagons were built at the same time for timber traffic and were rated at 25 tons. They were converted to aeroplane trucks in 1915 and were downrated to 20 tons. These became SR Diagram 1687 (see **Chapter 8**).

Most of the four-wheeled rail and sleeper wagons were flat vehicles with a combination of fixed and removable side stanchions, the design of which varied little over the years. An exception was SR Diagram 1799, which forms the subject of **Figure 36 (below)**. This was a convertible open/flat wagon, having detachable sides, enabling it to be used to carry ballast, rail or sleepers as required. Fifty were constructed by the Birmingham Railway Carriage & Wagon Company from 1897-99, LBSCR numbers being 8271-8300 and 8391-8410. All except No. 8292 survived at the Grouping, the remainder receiving SR numbers 64648-96. These were built on steel underframes along with Diagrams 1371, 1372, 1434 and the 'B' class open goods. Unlike all the rest, they stood the test of time and a few remained in the Engineer's fleet in the early 1950s. Perhaps they saw less rigorous service with the Engineer's Department than ordinary traffic wagons. There is little doubt that in former years wagon utilisation was very poor, much time being spent by the vehicles standing in goods yards rather than on the move, earning their keep.

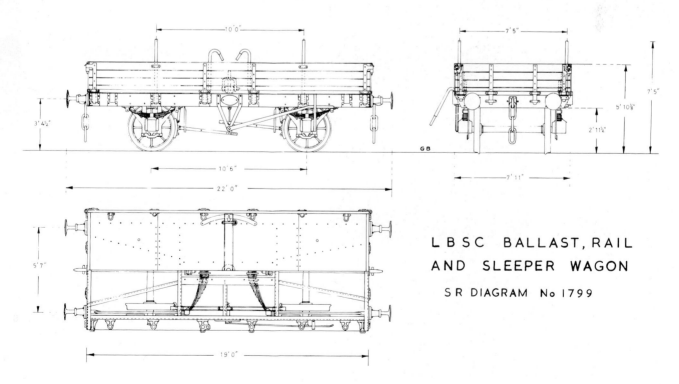

## LBSC BALLAST, RAIL AND SLEEPER WAGON
### SR DIAGRAM No 1799

**Figure 36**

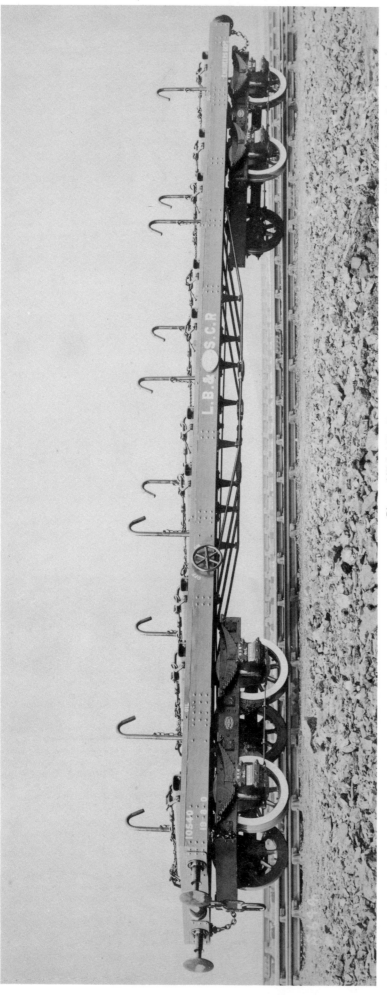

**Plates 117 & 118** Two views of wagon No. 10540 as delivered in 1904. The larger plate shows the side stanchions in the 'travelling' position, and the smaller plate shows them in the 'unloading' position. The rails could then be slid down to track level without risk of damage to the wagon.

*Hurst, Nelson & Co.*

For carrying 45ft. rails, twelve 30 ton (later 20 ton) bogie rail wagons were ordered from Hurst, Nelson and Company in 1903. These were delivered in the following year and remained the property of the Engineer's Department for their entire working lives. Three more similar wagons were completed at the same time and were intended for the conveyance of timber, being described as 25 ton bogie timber trucks. These were allocated to the Traffic Department. In detail, both versions appear to have been more the product of the builder than of the LBSCR, and they were amongst the earliest LBSCR wagons to have oil-lubricated axleboxes, this feature not being generally adopted until 1905. The Company considered them as 'exceptionally constructed wagons' and, as such, were subject to the operating restrictions detailed on **page 56**. LBSCR numbers of the rail wagons were 10540-51 (later SR Nos. 64726-37). All were down-rated to 20 tons in 1915 but were uprated to 21 tons in 1938. The timber trucks were LBSCR Nos. 10552-4 and became SR property as aeroplane trucks Nos. 61079-81.

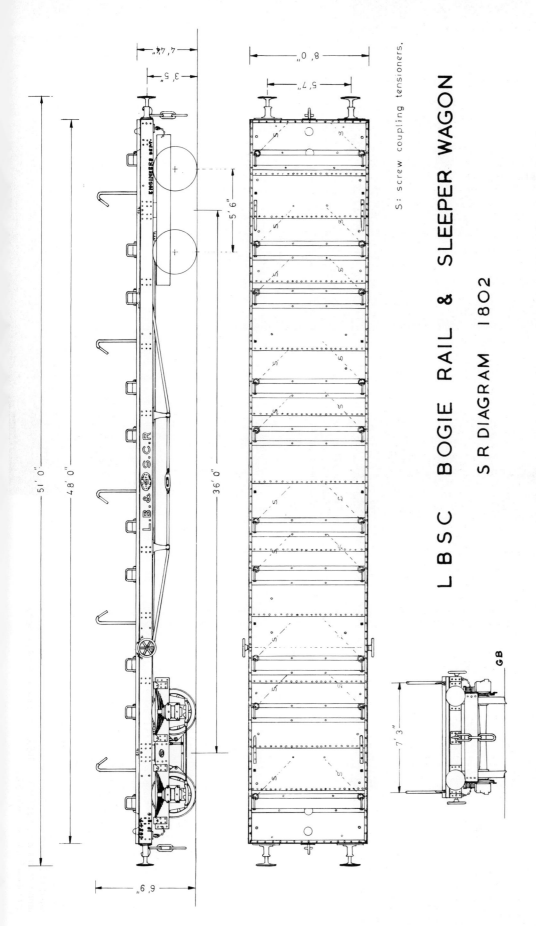

S: screw coupling tensioners.

# LBSC BOGIE RAIL & SLEEPER WAGON

## S R DIAGRAM 1802

**Figure 37** A drawing of the bogie rail wagon as built. The bogie timber trucks differed in detail as according to the 1910 LBSCR diagrams these had only four bolsters, spaced at 12ft. 0in. centres. Only four pairs of side stanchions were carried, positioned just outside each bolster. Regrettably, the authors are unable to locate any photographs of the timber trucks in their original form.

**Plate 119** Six wagons to Diagram 1802 were modified in 1952 for carrying long welded rails, with which the Southern Region was then experimenting. These were allocated SR Diagram 1803, the conversion simply involving repositioning of bolsters and the addition of through vacuum pipes. No. DS64731 was photographed at Eastleigh Works, circa 1960, probably awaiting scrapping. Note that self-contained buffers have also been fitted.

*R. E. Lacy*

Most of the LBSCR bogie rail wagons survived until the late 1950s, some being labelled 'Return to Angerstein Wharf' (ex-SECR) in 1938. The final examples of both diagrams were withdrawn in 1961.

The LBSCR points and crossing wagon, Diagram 44, was a long wheelbase flat wagon with one plank drop sides and four pairs of side stanchions. LBSCR records state them to be 31ft. 0in. long over headstocks, but the Southern Railway service stock register records this dimension as 31ft. 2in. No SR diagram appears to have been allocated but SR numbers were 352s-357s in the departmental stock list. Most were withdrawn between 1929 and 1934 but one remained in Signal Department use until 1938, usually being found at Wimbledon Yard. Once again, no photographs of these wagons are known to the authors.

The more usual design of LBSCR rail and sleeper wagon is illus-trated opposite in **Plate 120** and **Figure 38**. At least three varieties were extant at the Grouping. Diagram 1798 was, in effect, a shorter version of the double bolster wagon, having four fixed side stanchions arranged in two pairs at 9ft. 8in. centres. The 1910 LBSCR diagram describes these vehicles as 8 ton points wagons, but the diagram itself is identical to the later Southern Railway issue. Diagram 1800 was similar but had a centrally-mounted bolster and two removable side stanchions in addition to the four fixed ones. Both these designs had timber underframes, but the final type, SR Diagram 1801, was an updated version on a steel underframe, built during 1920/21 by the Metropolitan Carriage, Wagon & Finance Company. Both types were allocated the same LBSCR diagram number but were separated by the Southern Railway. Dimensionally both types were identical. Numbering details of these are as follows:

| SR Diagram | SR Numbers | LBSCR Numbers | Notes |
|---|---|---|---|
| 1800 | 64697-64705 | 3786-9/94-98 | |
| 1801 | 64706-64725 | 11095-11114 | These vehicles carry the highest numbers allocated to LBSCR goods wagons |

In underframe detail, Diagram 1801 was very similar to the open goods wagons built by Metropolitan at the same time, and are most unusual in that they are the only LBSCR wagons to have been fitted with Morton brakes.

At this point it may be worth recording those LBSCR diagram numbers extant in 1917 which, for various reasons, are outside the scope of our study. They are as below.

| LBSCR 1917 Diagram No. | Vehicle Type |
|---|---|
| 48 | Workshop van (ex-Stroudley six-wheeled passenger brake van) |
| 51 | Truck for pneumatic riveting (Engineer's Department) |
| 52 and 53 | Electric petrol inspection cars (Engineer's Department) |
| 54 | Gas holder wagons (several different types) |
| 55 | Tar tanks (several different types) |
| 56 | Mess and tool vans (several different types) |
| 57 | Breakdown cranes (several different types) |
| 59 | Stores vans (several different types) |
| 35, 36 and 50 | Not allocated |

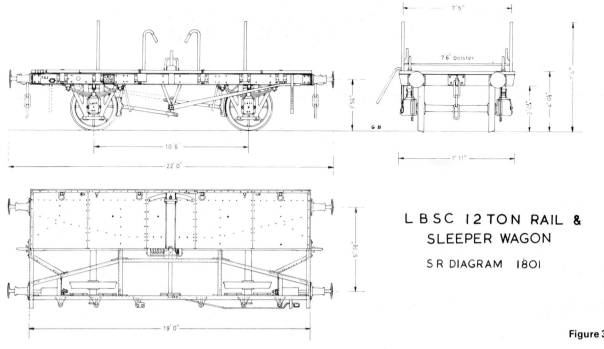

**LBSC 12 TON RAIL & SLEEPER WAGON**

**SR DIAGRAM 1801**

**Figure 38**

**Plate 120** Diagram 1801, rail and sleeper wagon No. 11114, the highest numbered LBSCR wagon. This later became SR No. 64725 and survived until April 1958. It was labelled 'Return to Angerstein Wharf' in May 1938. Note the very small lettering, the smallest size used by the LBSCR, the Company initials being just 2¾ in. high.

*W. O. Steel Collection*

**Examples of numbering (for full SR details refer to Appendix 1)**

| SR Diagram | SR Number | LBSCR Number | Date Built | With-drawn | Brake Gear | Notes |
|---|---|---|---|---|---|---|
| 1798 | 64645 | 7134 | 1891 | 6/35 | – | Brake gear details not recorded |
| 1798 | 64646 | 7136 | 1891 | 5/36 | – | Brake gear details not recorded |
| 1799 | 64690 | 8404 | 1897 | 1/54 | DB | Stencilled 'Return to Angerstein Wharf' 1938 |
| 1799 | 64694 | 8408 | 1897 | 11/52 | DB | Stencilled 'Return to Angerstein Wharf' 1938 |
| 1800 | 64698 | 3787 | 1894 | 5/34 | – | Brake gear details not recorded |
| 1800 | 64702 | 3795 | 1894 | 4/35 | – | Brake gear details not recorded |
| 1801 | 64708 | 11097 | 1921 | 7/60 | M | |
| 1801 | 64714 | 11103 | 1921 | 7/58 | M | Stencilled 'Return to Angerstein Wharf' 1938 |
| 1802 | 64726 | 10540 | 1904 | 6/58 | SC | |
| 1802 | 64735 | 10549 | 1904 | 4/61 | SC | |
| 1803 | 64732 | 10546 | Reb. 1952 | BR | SC | Ex-Diagram 1802. Vacuum pipes |
| 1803 | 64733 | 10547 | Reb. 1952 | 5/61 | SC | Ex-Diagram 1802. Vacuum pipes |
| – | 352s | 7829 | 1901 | 11/34 | – | Ex-LBSCR Diagram 44. SR departmental stock |
| – | 356s | 7838 | 1901 | 7/38 | – | Ex-LBSCR Diagram 44. SR departmental stock |

# Chapter 10
# Goods Department Travelling Cranes

The LBSCR operated about a dozen of these travelling cranes, a few more than the LSWR. Considering the slightly smaller system this probably indicates that fewer goods yards were equipped with static cranes. The following list summarises those cranes which became SR property in 1923, details being taken from the Southern Railway service stock register. Unfortunately, this does not detail the cranes as well as it does for ex-LSWR vehicles, such details as dimensions and allocations being omitted. The LBSCR allocated Diagram No. 58 for all travelling cranes, and Diagram No. 60 for crane wagons, i.e. match trucks.

| SR Number | LBSCR Number | Capacity (Tons) | Manufactured by | Date Built | No. of Wheels | Type | Withdrawn | Match Truck |
|---|---|---|---|---|---|---|---|---|
| 303s | 2 | - | Kirkstall Forge | 1878 | 6 | - | Pre-1946 | None |
| 304s | 4 | 5 | Booth Bros. | 1903 | 4 | Hand | - | 304sm |
| 305s | 5 | 5 | Booth Bros. | 1903 | 4 | Hand | - | 305sm |
| 306s | 6 | - | T. Smith | 1891 | 4 | Hand | 11/36 | 306sm |
| 307s | 7 | 10 | Booth Bros. | 1900 | 6 | Hand | - | 307sm |
| 308s | 8 | 10? | Booth Bros. | 1900 | 4 | Hand | 1/46 | 308sm |
| 309s | 9 | - | Booth Bros. | 1900 | 4 | Hand | 10/44 | 309sm |
| 310s | 10 | 6 | Booth Bros. | 1900 | 4 | Hand | - | 310sm |
| 311s | 11 | 6 | Booth Bros. | 1900 | 4 | Hand | - | 311sm |
| 312s | 12 | 6 | Booth Bros. | 1900 | 4 | Hand | Match Truck 1/48 | 312sm |
| 317s | 18 | 10 | Booth Bros. | 1904 | 6 | Hand | - | 317sm |
| 318s | 19 | 10 | Booth Bros. | 1904 | 6 | Hand | 10/45 | 318sm |

Notes:
1. The SR service stock register makes no mention of LBSCR cranes Nos. 1, 3 and 13. Cranes Nos. 14-17 and from No. 20 upwards were allocated to the Locomotive Department or Engineer's Department.
2. All match trucks were purpose-built to operate with their cranes. In later years some were replaced by conversions from open wagons, bolster wagons or road vehicle trucks. After 1948 they were renumbered into the departmental series proper, and no longer carried the same number as the crane

**Plate 121** The only known photograph of a Goods Department crane in pre-Grouping livery, depicting 10 ton machine No. 19, at Newhaven, probably soon after it was delivered in 1904. Note the lettering on the match truck and the timber brake block. In later years the moving parts of the crane mechanism were encased by steel sheeting. LBSCR livery is presumed to be the standard grey colour as used on ordinary goods wagons.

*Lens of Sutton*

**Plate 122** A 5 ton Booth crane, No. 305s, together with its match truck, at Herne Bay in the 1930s. The steel protection casing around the gear wheels can easily be seen. The match truck carries two lockers in which are stored the various jacks, chocks, chains and other equipment necessary for the operation of the crane. Safe operation of these machines was a skilled job, and accidents in use were by no means unknown.

*T. A. Barry Collection*

**Plates 123 & 124** Two views of 10 ton crane No. 307s standing on the headshunt at Weybridge goods yard in 1939. It was delivered to the station in the local goods train, together with the adjacent LNER bogie bolster wagon, which was loaded with a transformer that was beyond the capacity of the station's static yard crane. When photographed, it had completed its task and was awaiting collection by the following day's pick-up goods. The crane has recently been overhauled and appears to be painted in either brown, black or red oxide livery, instead of the more usual light grey. The weight box, at the end opposite the jib, could be run out as a counterweight, whilst lifting was in progress. The lettering on the match truck reads 'Crane must not be used without uncoupling tender'. The crane itself carries a 'Return to . . .' instruction, but unfortunately this cannot be deciphered.

*F. Foote*

**Plate 125** Crane No. DS314 (Ex-LBSCR No. 15) in British Railways grey livery. This was originally allocated to the Mechanical Engineer's Department at Brighton, but is now the property of the outdoor machinery section, hence the letters ODM. This has been included to show a crane with lattice jib construction. Built by J. Jessop & Son of Leicester in 1891, it was a hand crane of 8 tons capacity. The match truck is not the original No. 314sm, but was converted from the underframe of Diagram 1369 open goods wagon No. 22493 in April 1945.

*Authors' Collection*

**Plate 126** A slightly later photograph of crane No. DS314 at Kemp Town, showing the opposite side. The match truck has now been re-numbered as DS3100, and does not appear to have been repainted, unlike the crane, which now sports BR grey with black number and lettering patches.

*T. A. Barry Collection*

# Chapter 11
## The Isle of Wight Companies

Three railways handed over rolling stock to the Southern Railway on the Isle of Wight. These were the Isle of Wight Railway, a concern roughly 14 miles long, running from Ryde to Ventnor with a branch from Brading to Bembridge; the Isle of Wight Central Railway, a 29 mile system radiating from the Island's capital of Newport; and the 12 mile long Freshwater, Yarmouth & Newport Railway.

The traffic was entirely agricultural or domestic in character, and the Isle of Wight provides a good example of just how important the railways once were to the areas they served, when virtually everything was carried by train. On the Island, the goods traffic peaked in 1906 and in that year the IWR carried 59,211 tons of minerals, largely coal, and 7,240 tons of general goods. The IWCR, which at that time was also working the FY&NR, carried no less than 137,709 tons of minerals, and 62,427 tons of general goods, the latter figure reflecting

the amount of traffic originating from the merchants of Newport. As you will see from **Table A** on **page 93**, the three companies owned no less than 580 goods and departmental wagons in 1922, a total which reflects just one of the problems of running an island railway, where everything arrives by boat. The trouble was that neither the IWR quays at St. Helen's or the Central's wharf on the Medina had very much storage capacity, and so whenever a boat arrived, there had always to be enough empty wagons on hand in order to clear it. Coal, as always, made up by far the greatest proportion of the railway's traffic, and here the problem was exasperated by the ever increasing size of the colliers, and the length of time that the loaded wagons frequently stood about before they were unloaded. **Plate 127** well illustrates a very common sight.

### The Isle of Wight Railway

Taking the Island's railways in the order in which the Southern Railway renumbered their wagons, we find that the IWR was a modestly profitable and well-run little railway, serving the four main resorts of Ryde, Sandown, Shanklin and Ventnor, and together these towns were large enough to provide the railway with a healthy goods traffic. Of the Company's various wagons, approximately 126 had been built for it by the Oldbury Carriage & Wagon Co., 25 came new from an unknown manufacturer, 20 more were absorbed from the Brading Harbour & Railway Co., and a further 30 were purchased second-hand. All the others were built by Ryde, and most of those already mentioned were also 'rebuilt' there; a term used by Ryde to cover anything from a modest overhaul to the construction of a new wagon fitted with second-hand ironwork. There was a definite style to Ryde's work, but design was not their strong point, and many of the newer wagons were no more than enlarged copies of what they replaced.

Of the 189 open wagons, it can be said that a four plank side, given a height of 3ft., was very common. Combined with a width of 7ft. 2in., there were 4 at 18ft. long, 65 at 17ft. and 10 at 15ft. There were a further 40 at 15ft., but these were 7ft. 9in. wide. Eight were two plank dropsides, built on the underframes of old carriages, and the remainder reflected their early origins with dimensions of 13ft. x 7ft. 2in. x 2ft. 6in. or similar.

The IWR numbered its wagons in the order it purchased or built them. Rebuilds or replacements were normally of the same type, and took the number of the wagon they replaced. The brake vans and cranes each had a separate number series of their own. Many of the earlier wagons were of 6 or 9 tons capacity, and the reuse of old wheel sets resulted in this low rating for some of the newer wagons. Otherwise they were generally of 10 ton, 12 ton, or in six cases, 15 ton capacity.

There is a great deal of doubt about the Island railway's wagon liveries, and in the absence of any specifications there is not much to go on. The IWR wagon livery was, in later years, definitely chocolate brown, with the ironwork picked out in black, but this is thought to date only from about 1905, and beyond that we can only guess that slate grey may have been used. In 1904, the IWR purchased 20 second-hand wagons, Nos. 182-201, and these were known as the 'blue wagons', so one might guess that this was their former private owner livery. The wagons were lettered 'IWR' in approximately 12in. high characters. This practice is thought to date back to at least 1893, but it was not generally used until some years later, and as wagon No. 18 in **Plate 151** shows, a small letter style was still to be seen in 1919.

**Plate 127** Medina Wharf Sidings in 1930. There are approximately 90 loaded wagons in this picture, which describes better than words the problems of a railway which depended on the uncertain arrival of coal boats. Even those sailing barges could carry enough coal to fill 10 to 15 wagons, and the colliers 50 to 100. Looking at the wagons, No. 27912, in the middle foreground, was formerly IWR No. 152, built in 1912 and was destined to become loco. coal wagon No. 64348 in 1931. One of the earlier 64XXXs is also in the picture, as are two other Island wagons, but all the other open wagons which can be identified are Brighton-type five plank open wagons to SR Diagram 1364, including three with round ends. The wharf itself can just be made out in the top left-hand corner, where two former IWCR water tanks can be seen under the collier's wheel house.

*Authors' Collection*

**Plate 128** One of the authors first used this photograph in 1971, and it has appeared in print several times since, but we make no apologies for including it, as it is simply the best photograph we know of a pre-Grouping Isle of Wight coal train. In fact, the picture was taken in August 1923, but it shows no Southern influence; the locomotive carries the IWCR goods train headcode of a lamp over each buffer. The 'Terriers' were Class B in the Central's power rating, and the load of ten mineral wagons and a brake van was the maximum one of these engines was allowed to take between Newport and Ryde. The train was photographed near Smallbrook, and would seem to be carrying coal for Ryde gasworks. The train consists of two IWCR five plank open wagons, seven IWR four planks, and one IWR two plank dropside. The first wagon, IWR No. 45, is of particular interest, as it was one of the few genuine coal trucks on the Island at this time with a top through plank. The wagon was rated to carry 12 tons, and was officially a Ryde rebuild of 1905, but its length of 17ft. gives it away as a 'new' wagon of that date, incorporating the ironwork of an older wagon. The width was 7ft. 1½ in., and the height was 3ft. The original IWR No. 45 had dumb buffers, and so presumably it was decided that its replacement could manage with them also. Although the photograph cannot show it, the wagon is fitted with single block brakes on both sides, Ryde's thrifty answer to the Board of Trade's requirement to fit either-side brakes. The wagon was renumbered to 27953 in August 1927, and was withdrawn in June the following year. The next wagon is IWCR No. 220. It was one of thirteen similar wagons owned by the Central, it was built by the Bristol Wagon Co., and was one of forty coal wagons purchased second-hand in 1898 from the Bute Works Supply Co. The dimensions are, in the form described previously, 15ft. x 7ft. 4in. x 2ft. 11in. This wagon never carried a SR number and like IWR No. 45 it was withdrawn in June 1928. The last wagon is one of nine similar two plank dropsides, built by the IWR between 1915 and 1920 on the underframes of withdrawn carriages. They were all 7ft. 7in. wide with sides 1ft. 6in. deep, but their lengths varied. Six were 21ft. long, and the remainder a few inches shorter. They were only rated to carry 6 tons, and although the Southern renumbered two of them as ballast wagons, they had all been withdrawn by May 1928. Finally, the brake van is either IWCR No. 2 or 3, described in full on **page 87**.

*Authors' Collection*

**Plate 129** In 1903, the IWR built the first of its rather unusual 17ft. open wagons. It is believed that 65 were built in all, two of 9 tons capacity, 53 of 10 tons, and 10 of 12 tons. IWR No. 45 in **Plate 128** is typical of the earlier wagons, but most were normal opens with self-contained spring buffers, which were themselves features of later IWR practice. Some of these wagons had a wheelbase of 9ft. 9in., but most are believed to have been about 11ft. as shown in **Figure 39**. They were nearly all, whatever their other variations, 7ft. 1½ in. or 7ft. 2in. wide, and 3ft. deep. In 1929, Mr MacLeod, then the Mechanical Assistant for the Isle of Wight, decided to retain eight of these wagons to carry locomotive coal and ashes; these were Nos. 64393-400. In 1931, a further four were required, Nos. 64348-51, but of these, one, No. 64349, was a 15ft. wagon (formerly SR 27911/IWR 151), otherwise it was very similar. Their livery was the standard SR brown, but the lettering layout was one of several specially drafted by Mr MacLeod during his time on the Island. Most of these wagons survived until about 1959, when they were replaced by Brighton five plank wagons. In their later days the former IWR wagons exhibited many detail modifications, including five plank sides, Brighton doors, and altered strapping.

*Authors' Collection*

**Plate 130** IWR No. 29, photographed at Ningwood in June 1928, was renumbered SR 27838 three months later, and was withdrawn the following March. According to SR records, this 9 ton wagon was rebuilt at Ryde in 1922, and the wide spacing of the solebars, as evidenced by the buffer backing plate, show it to have wheel sets manufactured by the Oldbury Carriage & Wagon Co. in the 1870s; the axleboxes are also of this vintage. The wagon's dimensions, however, were recorded as 15ft. over headstocks x 7ft. 9in. over sides x a side height of 3ft. However, as none of these early wagons agree with these particular dimensions, we conclude that this vehicle was built around the turn of the century, utilising the ironwork of the original IWR No. 29. The single door stop was a very common feature of IWR open wagons, as are the little cast-iron load and label plates. The wagon has two sets of double brakes, the second set having probably been added in the 1922 'rebuild'. No. 29 portrays the standard IWR lettering and number layout very well, and was presumably in a faded brown livery with black ironwork. The wagon to the left is either SR No. 28146/IWCR No. 40, or SR No. 28179/IWCR No. 158, these being the only two IWCR 10 tonners with a tare weight of 4-6-0. The wagon on the right is one of the Brighton five planks, No. 28335, built at Lancing in September 1925, and transferred to the Island in April or May 1927.

*H. F. Wheeller*

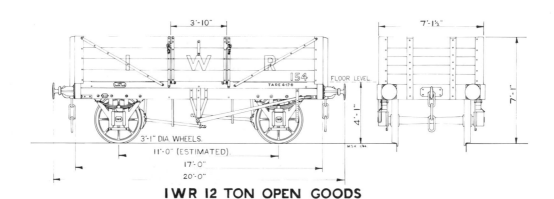

**IWR 12 TON OPEN GOODS**

**Figure 39**

**Plate 131** One of the earlier IWR covered goods vans, in 1960, grounded as a store in Ryde St. John's Yard. On the fourth plank down on the left-hand side, the initials 'IWR' in the small lettering style are just visible.

*A. Blackburn*

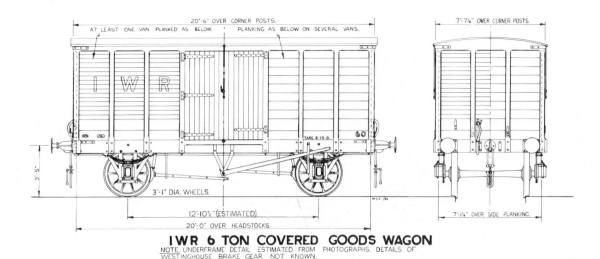

20'-6" OVER CORNER POSTS.

AT LEAST ONE VAN PLANKED AS BELOW. PLANKING AS BELOW ON SEVERAL VANS.

7'-7¾" OVER CORNER POSTS.

3'-5"

3'-1" DIA. WHEELS.

TARE 5-19-0.

12'-10½" (ESTIMATED)

20'-0" OVER HEADSTOCKS.

7'-1¼" OVER SIDE PLANKING.

## IWR 6 TON COVERED GOODS WAGON

NOTE. UNDERFRAME DETAIL ESTIMATED FROM PHOTOGRAPHS. DETAILS OF
WESTINGHOUSE BRAKE GEAR NOT KNOWN.

**Figure 40** We would like to know more about the IWR covered goods vans, but although all twelve were sold out of service in 1928, we have only found one to measure. By contrast, at least six of those they replaced were still in use as huts some thirty years after they were withdrawn, and from these we can say that the later vehicles were, in many respects, copies of the vans they replaced, with the exception that they were generally 2ft. longer. Our composite drawing shows, on the left of the centre line, one particular vehicle which is thought to have been IWR No. 60 or 61. On the right-hand side we have drawn what we believe to have been a more common version, although it may not be accurate to the last inch. The body side planks are wider than the solebar by about ¾in. on either side. Unfortunately the underframe was too badly defaced for us to draw any definite conclusions as to what the wheelbase had been, but the one drawn is the most probable. The wheel sets were almost certainly those of the original vans they replaced. We have drawn the normal type of self-contained buffer used by the IWR, but they may well have carried a heavier cast-iron version similar to those seen on the 2 ton crane illustrated in **Plate 140**. All these vans were provided with Westinghouse brakes, but in the complete absence of any information as to how these were arranged, we have shown handbrakes only. We must also admit to knowing very little about the IWR's three cattle trucks. The only known photograph of one in later years is not suitable for reproduction or detailed interpretation, but shows a vehicle with cross bracing on the end but, rather unusually, none at the side. Their main dimensions were recorded by the SR as 14ft. 3in. x 8ft. x 7ft. 4in. All three were withdrawn in March 1927.

**Plate 132** This is not a very clear photograph, but it is the only one we have which shows one of the later IWR covered goods wagons. The third and fourth wagons in the train are two plank dropside rebuilds, loaded with beer barrels, and the photograph was taken at Ventnor in 1920.

*Authors' Collection*

**Plate 133** IWR goods brake van No. 1. This vehicle dates right back to the opening of the railway in 1864, and it was built by the Oldbury Railway Carriage & Wagon Co. Ltd., the centrally-placed guard's accommodation being typical of the many early goods brake vans built by the Birmingham carriage & wagon industry. The photograph is undated, but almost certainly shows the van as it was rebuilt at Ryde in 1916. The 3½in. tongue and groove boarding is typical of Ryde's practice at this time, and you will notice that it was also used on a covered goods van. The five link coupling provides further evidence of the vehicle's great age. The main dimensions were recorded as 17ft. 1in. x 7ft. 9in. x 6ft. 4in. It had a wheelbase of 9ft. This van was renumbered 56033 in June 1924, and was replaced by an LSWR road van, No. 56049, in December 1928. The open wagon is a typical IWR four plank. Unlike the wagon shown in **Plate 130**, however, it has normal wheel sets with a width over solebars of about 6ft. 9in., giving the common IWR width of 7ft. 2in. over side sheets. The length is probably 17ft., but there were very similar 15ft. examples.

*R. C. Riley Collection*

**Plate 134** In 1879 the IWR purchased a second goods brake van. By its general appearance in later years we would guess that it had not changed very much in its life, although a very poor photograph, taken in 1920, almost certainly shows large dumb buffer blocks, bolted on to its headstocks in place of the self-contained buffers shown, rather like a contractor's shunting engine. These may, however, have been a temporary alteration. As can be seen from both the photograph and **Figure 41**, it has almost nothing in common with No. 1, except for the rather skimpy handrails. It was given the number 56034 in March 1924, and was further renumbered 472S in August 1932, when it was selected for use with the Engineer's Department weed killing train that was made up in that year from two old IWCR tanks (**see Plate 155**). It was used each spring for this purpose until 1948, when it was officially replaced by LSWR brake van No. 56054, renumbered 548S. In practice, any convenient van was used on the weed killing train in later years.

*Authors' Collection*

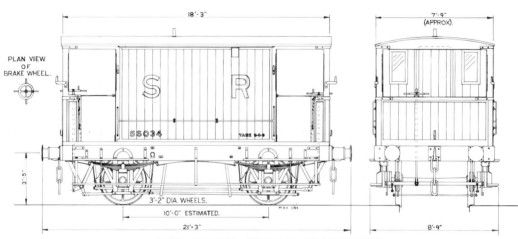

**IWR 9 TON GOODS BRAKE VAN**

**Figure 41**

**Plate 135** A very interesting photograph, taken at Ventnor in June 1928 by Mr Hubert Wheeller, who was one of the few people at that time to realise the interest of goods stock. The wagon on the extreme left is an IWR bolster wagon in SR livery, whilst next to it is another, IWR No. 89, as rebuilt by Ryde in 1920. The dimensions are 15ft. x 8ft. x 9in. Notice the very low bolster height and the double-sided single block brakes. IWCR No. 150 is credited to the 'North Central', but this company is thought to have been a finance house, and the wagon was quite possibly built at Newport. Its dimensions are 15ft. x 7ft. 4in x 2ft. 11in. It has a one-side double brake and is typical of the later IWCR open wagons in every detail. The wagon was never given its SR number, and the livery is almost certainly black, with the exception of the door and one quarter board, which are probably SR brown. No. 26142 is one of the first twenty LBSC-designed open wagons sent to the Island in 1924, all of which had round ends; its tare at this time was 5-14-2. Note the fixed hand-crane in the background. The IWR built up quite a considerable amount of container traffic with the mainland, and the stations at Ryde, Sandown, Shanklin and Ventnor were all equipped with similar cranes to handle the containers.

*H. F. Wheeller*

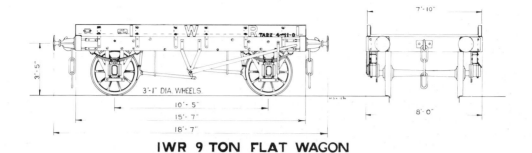

**IWR 9 TON FLAT WAGON**

**Figure 42** This portrays IWR 9 ton flat wagon No. 1. We have chosen to draw this particular wagon because we have several good photographs of it, and it is very typical of the others. You will see that apart from the absence of a bolster, it is very similar indeed to the bolster wagon shown in **Plate 135**. The end elevation shows well the wide spacing of the Oldbury wheel sets, and you will notice how Ryde took advantage of this to build a very simple wagon that is nevertheless wide enough to accommodate a container without the complications of specially-cut crib rails. There were no knees or packings, the solebars have simple pieces of strip plate bolted to them, and on the back of these is fitted the side rail. Note that the two plates either side of the 'vee' hanger were spaced as drawn. It must be said that Ryde had little idea of the finer points of carriage and wagon design. This particular wagon was allocated the number 1021, but that may not have been carried. In November 1931, it was selected to become the Ryde Works flat wagon No. 568S. In recognition of it having been the last wagon to have been shopped by the IWR, Mr MacLeod had it relettered IWR, but only on one side, that being the side furthest from the running line, and hence the eyes of visiting mainland authority! In this form it survived until about 1952, when it was replaced by a cut-down Brighton covered goods wagon.

**Plate 136** This IWR carriage truck was goods wagon No. 76, but the Southern considered it to be a passenger stock vehicle, and gave it the number 4380. In June 1930, it was taken into departmental stock as a boiler trolley and renumbered 439S. The photograph was taken in 1930 and shows it loaded with the A1 type boiler taken out of 'Terrier' No. W10. As a passenger vehicle it must have been fitted, and it will be noticed that it still retains a tail lamp bracket, not to mention the side chains and wheel bar brackets. **Figure 43** shows the wagon as modified to become a boiler trolley with a hole cut in the floor to accommodate the boiler's firebox. Later, a bracket was provided to support the front of the boiler. The wagon was used to carry locomotive boilers between Ryde and St. Helen's Quay, where they were loaded into barges by a big, fixed, 10 ton hand crane, for onward transit to Eastleigh Works, Ryde not being equipped to carry out heavy boiler work. This was not the wagon's only use, for there is a photograph in existence which was taken about 1931, and this shows it loaded with a steamroller at Newport.

*Authors' Collection*

**Figure 43**

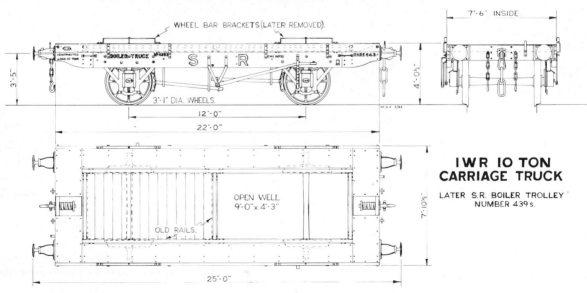

**IWR 10 TON CARRIAGE TRUCK**

LATER S.R. BOILER TROLLEY NUMBER 439 S.

**Plate 137** In 1906 Ryde built two 15 ton tar tanks; the railway's goods stock then totalled 201 vehicles, so they were numbered 202-3. They had wooden underframes 18ft. long, and these were probably similar to four 15 ton open wagons that were also built in 1906, except that they are thought to have had dumb buffers. The tanks were 17ft. long overall, and were 6ft. 1⅝in. in diameter; the tank end stock was 7ft. long. These tanks worked between the gasworks at Ryde and St. Helen's, and various other stations on the Island as required. In 1923 they were allocated the numbers 61381-2, and in 1929 the tanks were placed on the 18ft. underframes taken from two LSWR covered goods wagons. As such they were almost the only Island wagons to receive the distinction of an SR diagram, No. 1713. They are seen in this form in the photograph, and ran thus until 1947 when they were replaced by two LSWR engine tenders (**see Plate 163**). They are thought to have been the only SR revenue-earning tank cars, and their livery is not known to the authors, but black seems more likely than brown; perhaps the tanks were black and the solebars brown. It is not in our remit to deal with private owner wagons, but as the third wagon in the photograph is one of the few to run in the Island, a few words about them does not seem out of place. The biggest operator was the Vectis Stone Co., later a part of the Associated Portland Cement Co. They operated a total of 35 four plank end door open wagons, 30 'small' ones, quoted as being about the size of a Price & Reeves wagon, to be described later, and five larger ones. Besides these there was a small number of coal wagons operated from Brading Quay in the very early days, whilst Messrs Alexander Sharpe & Co. of Newport ran two timber trucks from about 1895 until they sold them to the IWCR in 1915. The tank in the photograph is very similar to one of at least two known to have been operated by 'Royal Daylight', and this one may also have been operated by them. Lastly, there was a very unusual private owner incline brake van, which belonged to the Ashey Marl-Pit line. We know of this because it was at one time reported as having been stolen by the IWCR! This list is not exhaustive and there may well have been other private owner wagons at various times.

*A. B. MacLeod*

**Plate 138** A later design of IWR axlebox as used from the turn of the century, here seen under one of the 12 ton open wagons. The spacing of the side spring shoes at 3ft. is unusual, 3ft. 6in. being normal RCH practice. Notice the lack of a crown and wing plates, the nuts simply being tightened up on washers; this was a feature of both IWR and IWCR practice. The label clip is modern.

*J. J. Davis*

**Plate 139** The IWR owned two travelling cranes, and the larger became SR No. 426S and was a 10 tonner, built in 1876 by James Taylor of Birkenhead. It is shown in the chalk siding at Brading, but it was officially allocated to the Operating Department at St. Helen's Quay. The carriage measured 15ft. over the end of its steel frame, but to each end of this there was bolted a 6½in. thick wooden headstock. The width over the dropped working platforms was 7ft. 6in., and the platforms themselves were 15ft. long x 2ft. 6in. wide. The pivot casting was approximately 6ft. 6in. in diameter at its base, and the wheelbase was 10ft. 6in. The crane itself had a maximum lifting radius of 20ft. The tail was approximately 8ft. 4in. from the pivot point, whilst the total length of the crane frame over the fulcrum radius was approximately 12ft. 7in., the whole being 7½ in. clear of the steel floor. The crane frames were 3ft. 4in. wide over their plate work, whilst the depth of the tail was 1ft. The overall height of the crane frame was approximately 6ft. 3in. The jib side plates were 1ft. 1in. deep at the bottom, and had a slight taper towards the head; the space between the jib sides was filled by a centrally-placed steel plate. We have no details of the original match truck, but the one shown was originally IWR open goods wagon No. 107, which was itself a 'rebuild' of 1906. This wagon became No. 426SM (skillet match) in 1927. The length was 17ft., width over soles 6ft. 8in., over sides 7ft. 1½in., and over headstocks 7ft. 7in. The wheelbase was 9ft. 9in., and the depth of the side totalled 1ft. 6in. In the 1930s, this wagon had two plank sides, but latterly three were used. The LBSCR grease axleboxes were fitted by the SR. Both the crane and its match truck were painted red oxide in SR days, and BR repainted them black in August 1950.

*A. Blackburn*

**Plate 140** No. 425S, the Isle of Wight Railway's 2 ton yard crane was built in 1865 by the Kirkstall Forge Co. of Leeds. Note the Oldbury C&W Company self-contained buffers and the five link coupling without a hook. This vehicle was used within Ryde Works Yard.

*A. Blackburn*

**Plate 141** SR No. 426SM at Ryde in the mid-1930s. Note the self-contained buffers mounted on packing, and the screw coupling. The van to the left is SR No. 46955, tare 6-17-0. SR No. 28277 to the right is tared 5-12-0.

*H. F. Wheeler*

**Plate 142** The former IWR wagon shop at Ryde.

*A. Blackburn*

**Plate 143 (Below Left)** A very interesting photograph taken on the South Quay at St. Helen's in the 1930s. The siding on the extreme left was known as the 'Carrier' road, and was built to serve the train ferry barge of that name. The Brighton bolster wagons were probably waiting to be loaded with rails. The steam crane on the left was fitted with buffers, and was capable of carrying out light shunting duties. It had only recently arrived at St. Helen's and was formerly used on Medina Wharf. One of the IWR tar tanks can be seen in the background, and a container is being unloaded from the steam coaster *Excelsior*.

*A. B. MacLeod*

**Plate 144 (Below)** This photograph was taken from the end of the Freshwater railway platform at Newport in 1920. There is a good mix of both IWR and IWCR open wagons to be seen, and some of the latter are black with large letters, others being grey with small letters. The open wagon standing second to the right of the van is a Freshwater wagon and the van itself is a passenger brake. The Island companies did not believe in carrying any spare stock on their books and frequently resorted to the use of a passenger brake van whenever a goods brake van was not available.

*Authors' Collection*

## The Isle of Wight Central Railway

The IWCR had its origins in the Cowes & Newport Railway. This little line was opened in 1862 and was very unusual, in that it only carried passenger traffic; the few wagons it possessed were ballast trucks. This line was joined in Newport in 1875 by the Ryde & Newport Railway. This company owned 23 open and 20 ballast wagons, and with these it commenced a goods train service; they were all obtained second-hand. Both these railways were worked by a Joint Committee from 1877, and in 1879 they opened a wharf on the Medina River, near Cowes. To handle the increased traffic, a total of 76 open and three covered goods wagons was obtained from the Oldbury C&W Co.

Meanwhile, a third railway was approaching Newport from the direction of Sandown. This was the Isle of Wight (Newport Junction) Railway. In 1877, it returned 18 wagons to the Board of Trade, and it is thought that at least some of these were built for the line by the Metropolitan Railway Carriage & Wagon Co. In 1877, these three railways were amalgamated to form the IWCR, and in that year it returned a total of 138 wagons.

The only repair facilities the Company possessed were those originally provided by the C&NR at Cowes. These were totally inadequate, and in 1891 they were replaced by a new workshop at Newport. The mineral and goods traffic had risen steadily every year since the opening of Medina Wharf, but despite this, the Company was never a financial success, and the 25 open wagons built by Messrs Harrison & Camm in 1897 were destined to be its last new purchases. Henceforth the steadily increasing traffic had to be catered for by second-hand purchases, of which there were roundly 140 spread over the next fifteen years. Rebuilds and reconstructions, however, were carried out by Newport, and many of these were virtually new wagons.

At the turn of the century, the railway was in trouble with the Board of Trade concerning the condition of its goods stock. At this time it was suffering from a lack of both operating and engineering expertise. Matters improved over the next few years, but an internal report, written in 1912, still found much to complain about. In that year, however, the Company obtained the services of Mr Russell Wilmot as General Manager. He was a very experienced railwayman, and under his leadership the Central finally became a very well-run railway.

Of the Company's 251 open wagons, no less than 224 were five planks, 10 of these were 16ft. long, 150 were 15ft. and 50 were 14ft. The remainder were almost every length you can think of between 13ft. 6in. and 16ft. Of the other open wagons, two were three plank dropsides, and the remainder dumb-buffered six planks, some 16ft. long, and others 14ft. 2in. long. Most of the Company's earlier second-hand purchases came from South Wales. Between the years 1904 and 1909, Great Eastern wagons were favoured, and from 1911-12 a large number of purchases were made from the Midland Railway.

The Central generally seems to have numbered its wagons in the order in which it purchased them, but the list is complicated by some attempt to renumber wagons of the same type together as, for example, in the case of the cattle trucks. The brake vans and cranes were numbered in their own separate series.

So far as livery is concerned, it is known that the ten wagons purchased from the Gloucester C&W Company in 1888 were painted brown with white letters shaded black. Later the wagons were painted grey with white lettering in the same style as shown in **Plate 145**. Some time prior to 1919, perhaps as early as 1909, the Company commenced painting its stock all over black with the large letters IWC normally spread across the full width of the wagon. This livery change was not complete by 1923 when, from photographic evidence, it would seem there remained a good few grey ones.

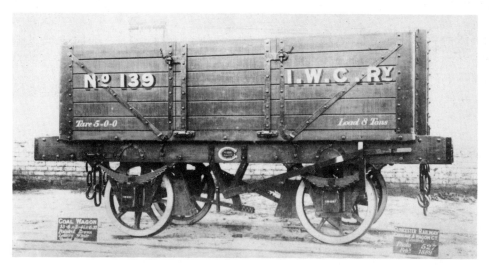

**Plate 145** This is one of only three official builder's photographs known of an Island wagon when new. It shows IWCR No. 139, and is one of ten purchased from the Gloucester Railway Carriage & Wagon Co. in 1889. It is a typical coal wagon of the 1860-80 period, but the design was decidedly dated by the time that this wagon was built, and the dumb buffers were probably accepted in order to save money. These wagons did not survive long enough to become Southern property.

*Authors' Collection*

**Plate 146** A view of locomotive No. W12 shunting the then recently-rebuilt Freshwater Yard at Newport in November 1928. The rather heavy-looking wagon next to the engine is No. 28049, formerly IWCR No. 129. This wagon was built at Newport, it has one set of double brakes, and it measured 14ft. x 7ft. 6in. x 2ft. 11in. The tare weight was 4-6-0, and it was withdrawn in July 1930. The remaining wagons are all to Diagram 1364, and make a useful comparison. Their dimensions are 15ft. 5in. x 7ft. 9in. x 2ft. 11in.

*H. C. Casserley*

**Plate 147** The IWCR five plank wagons, as found by Mr Wheeller in June 1928. **Top left** is SR No. 28210/IWCR No. 264 at Ventnor, one of four open wagons purchased second-hand from the Bute Works Supply Co. Cardiff, in 1900. The dimensions are 14ft. 10in. x 7ft. 4in. x 3ft. 1in. It has one set of double brakes, and it was withdrawn in July 1930. Notice the straps under the solebars and over the spring shoes. **Top right** at Freshwater, we have IWCR No. 68, with small lettering and the number on the same plank; it is probably painted grey. This wagon was one of some two dozen owned by the IWCR, and built by the firm of Stableford. The dimensions are 15ft. x 7ft. 9in. x 2ft. 11in. It was an 8 ton wagon, and it had one set of double brakes. According to the SR records, this wagon was renumbered in April 1928, but quite clearly it was not, and withdrawal followed later in the month, in which it was photographed. SR No. 28363, tare 5-14-2, was built at Lancing in May 1924 and reached the Island exactly three years later. **Bottom left** is IWCR No. 117, found at Newport with the later form of lettering, which would seem to be associated with the all-over black livery. It is another 8 ton wagon, this time credited to the British Wagon Company. The internal diagonal strapping is a very old-fashioned feature, and the wagon probably dates back to the 1880s. The cast-iron self-contained buffers are far more typical of Central practice than the pressed variety seen on SR No. 28210. Dimensions were 14ft. 8in. x 7ft. 4in. x 3ft. 2in. The narrow make up plank is unusual, and is identical to that found on an IWR wagon of which we have a photograph. From this, we guess that the carpenter concerned had changed railways. The wagon itself was probably built with four large side planks. No. 117 was also withdrawn later in the month. The wagon on the left is probably SR No. 27880/IWR No. 183, as rebuilt in 1920, 15ft. x 7ft. 9in. x 2ft. 6in., withdrawn April 1929. **Bottom right**. What a delightful and interesting picture; No. W8, possibly the Island's prettiest engine is here found working for the Permanent Way Department at the end of the new Freshwater line loop, then nearing completion at Newport. SR No. 28058/IWCR No. 159 was probably built at Newport. The dimensions are 14ft. 5in. x 7ft. 6in. x 2ft. 11in.; its tare was 4-9-0. It had one set of double brakes and was withdrawn in July 1930.

*H. F. Wheeller*

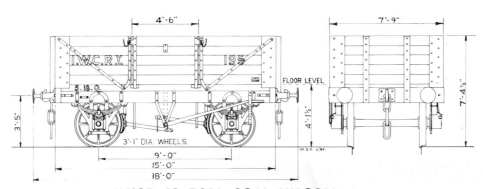

**Figure 44**

**IWCR 10 TON COAL WAGON**
IWCR Nº 195-219, BUILT BY HARRISON & CAMM Lᵀᴰ
IN 1897.

**Figure 44** This shows one of the 25 open wagons built for the IWCR in 1897 by Messrs Harrison & Camm, Nos. 195-219. These wagons were very typical of a large number of similar vehicles which the Central built or acquired second-hand in the next twenty years, except that their depth of 3ft. 3in. was 3in. more than the norm. To put these five plank open wagons in their proper perspective, we show **Figure 45**, a drawing of the 1889 RCH standard 8 ton coal wagon, for this is the specification drawing to which most of the second-hand examples, at least, were built. It should be mentioned that most Isle of Wight examples would have had a five plank drop door, and that none had end doors. The detail of the diagonal and knee strap joints, as shown on the drawing, is unusual; the simpler arrangement shown in **Figure 44** was more normal. Both the IWR and the IWCR had owned a number of end door wagons, but it is thought that none remained in this condition to become SR property.

Figure 45

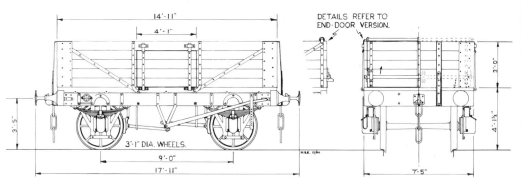

**STANDARD 8 TON OPEN GOODS WAGON (RCH SPECIFICATION) SEPTEMBER 1889**

**Plate 148** Locomotive No. W12 with a short goods train at Merstone Junction in June 1928. Next to the engine is one of the six former Midland Railway covered goods vans owned by the IWCR. These varied in their details, and it will be noticed that this one lacks the modified side sheeting shown on IWCR No. 324 in **Figure 46**. At least one other had normal side sheeting and a foot board. Towering above the van is one of the first three Brighton cattle trucks on the Island (Nos. 53374-6). Of the two open wagons, one is IWCR, the other probably Brighton, and so is the wagon on the other side of the platform. The brake van is the Midland vehicle shown in **Plate 151**. Although this is nothing to do with wagons, notice the Island practice of screwing down flat bottom rails straight on to the sleepers without the use of base plates. The screws pass through holes drilled in the foot of the rail.

*H. F. Wheeller*

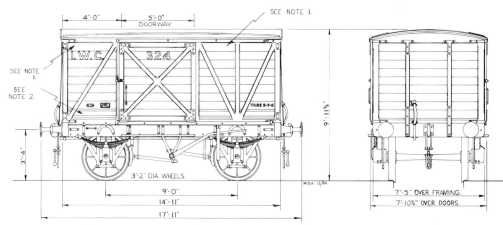

Figure 46

**IWCR 8 & 10 TON COVERED GOODS** EX-MIDLAND RAILWAY VEHICLES.
NOTE I. TOP SIDE PLANK REMOVED BY IWCR & VANS USED AS VENTILATED VEHICLES.
NOTE 2. BOTTOM SIDE PLANK REPLACED BY NARROWER TIMBER BY IWCR. WESTINGHOUSE PIPE AND SCREW COUPLINGS FITTED BY IWCR.

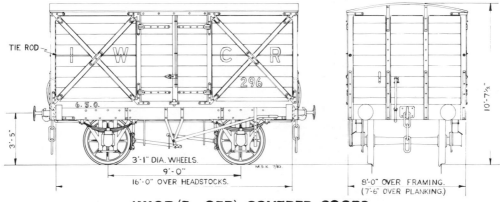

**IWCR (Ex-GER) COVERED GOODS**

**Figure 47** This shows one of the two dozen or so covered goods wagons purchased from Messrs Frazer & Son, the well-known second-hand rolling stock supplier. These vans were acquired over the years 1904-9, and most. if not all of them, came from the Great Eastern Railway, but they were by no means identical. We have shown what is believed to have been the most common IWCR lettering style for these wagons, but one at least, possibly No. 274 or 277, was still running in 1929 in IWC livery with the small letters 'iwc' in the middle of the second plank down in the top quarter of the left-hand side. The number was probably in the same location on the right-hand side, but this cannot be confirmed.

**Plate 149** SR cattle truck No. 53385, formerly IWCR No. 43, one of six or seven ex-GER, purchased by the Central between 1904 and 1909. It is thought that they were all similar in their details, but only one other, No. 53384/IWCR No. 42, was exactly the same as to its dimensions. Note the large blocks on which the buffers are packed out to suit the screw couplings. The truck is Westinghouse fitted, and it was no doubt this feature which made the GER vehicles attractive to the IWCR. A drawing of No. 53385 is shown in **Figure 48**. No. 53385 had the distinction, along with No. 27914/IWR No. 156, a 17ft. open wagon, and No. 28802/IWCR No. 76, a 16ft. open wagon, of being the last three Island wagons to remain in revenue-earning service, all three being withdrawn on 27th January 1934.

*Authors' Collection*

**Figure 48**

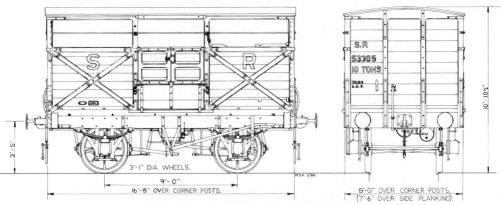

**IWCR 10 TON MEDIUM CATTLE WAGON (Ex-GER)**

**Plate 150** Yet another fine picture by Mr Wheeller, this time taken in June 1928 at Ningwood. On the left is IWR timber truck No. 93, and on the right we have one of the Brighton bolster wagons which had only arrived on the Island in the previous month. It is, however, the two IWC bolster wagons, Nos. 321/2 that we are particularly interested in. Together with a third, No. 320, they were purchased from the MR in July 1911. They never carried their SR numbers (59028-30), and all three were destined to be withdrawn three months after this picture was taken. The last wagon in the picture is a former IWR four plank.

*H. F. Wheeller*

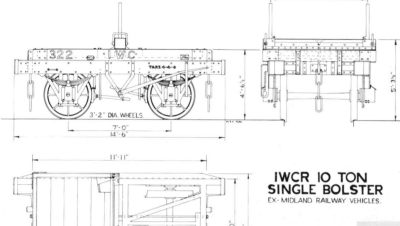

### IWCR 10 TON SINGLE BOLSTER
EX-MIDLAND RAILWAY VEHICLES.

**Figure 49**

**Figure 49** shows IWC No. 322. In addition to these three vehicles, the IWCR owned, in 1922, two double bolster wagons purchased from the GCR, two former LBSCR batten trucks, Nos. 335-6, something of very similar dimensions, built either by the Metropolitan Railway or the Metropolitan Railway Carriage & Wagon Co., No. 283, and lastly No. 353, the survivor of two former private owner timber trucks purchased in 1915 from the Newport firm of Sharp & Co.

*H. F. Wheeller*

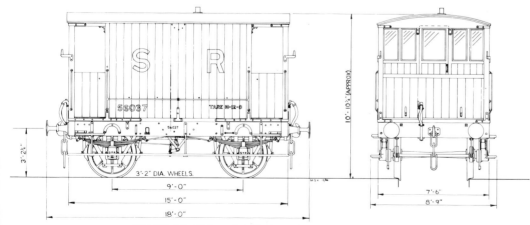

**Figure 50**

### IWCR 10 TON GOODS BRAKE VAN
AS REBUILT FROM MIDLAND RAILWAY VEHICLE IN 1930.
S.R. DIAGRAM 1588.

**Plate 151** This very interesting photograph was first reproduced in the April 1919 edition of the magazine *Railway and Travel Monthly*, and it shows a short goods train at Sandown. The nearest vehicle is a former Midland Railway brake van, purchased from that company in July 1911, and featured in **Figure 50**, as rebuilt by the Southern Railway in 1930. As such, it was the only Island wagon, apart from the tar tanks, to receive an SR diagram, No. 1588. The open wagon with a wooden sheet bar is IWR No. 18, as rebuilt by Ryde in 1902. Its dimensions were 15ft. x 7ft. 9in. x 2ft. It is of 9 ton capacity and has a single brake block and lever on the far side. Although many of the early IWR open wagons had a low 'D' end, true round-ended wagons, such as this, were rare on the Island. The covered goods van is one of the former GER vehicles, purchased between 1904 and 1909 and drawn in **Figure 47**.

*Authors' Collection*

**Plate 152** This fine photograph was taken at Newport in 1933, and shows, from left to right, No. 56048, one of the former Diagram 1541 vans of LSWR origin (**see Figure 54**), No. 56037, the Ryde rebuild of IWCR No. 5, and No. 56054, a standard Diagram 1541 wagon. Note that all three have inset bottom footboards required by the Isle of Wight loading gauge.

*A. B. MacLeod*

**Plate 153** This vehicle was IWCR 'goods brake and tranship van No. 3'. Together with its twin, No. 2, they represented Newport's most ambitious wagon work. The wheels and ironwork are those of a Stroudley brake van, but the body is believed to be new, although it must be said that the Central owned at least one almost identical covered goods wagon, so it may be a rebuild. These vans have quite a number of details in common with No. 438s (**see page 89**) so one way or another it looks as if they were all built by Newport Works. Photographs show these brake vans all over the Central system, and in 1928 one was working on the Bembridge branch. No. 2 was withdrawn in June 1928, but No. 3 was converted into a mess and tool van and served on into the early 1950s.

*Authors' Collection*

**Figure 51** We have built up this drawing from two side views and several known dimensions, so we cannot vouch for its accuracy to the last inch. In particular, we have had to guess at the construction of the balcony end. We know the end boarding was flush to the inner frames of the end uprights, and we think that the timbers were vertical. Again, we think it likely that Newport probably used one of the old Stroudley side doors in the end. This is the only drawing in these volumes that we have had to guess at in this way, but it is a very interesting vehicle and it seemed a shame not to include it.

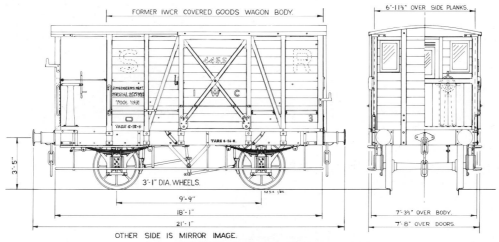

**IWCR 7 TON GOODS BRAKE AND TRANSHIP VAN**

**Plate 154** Showing not a trace of its identity is SR No. 443S, formerly SR No. 61383/IWCR No. 140. This tank was one of two purchased from the Bute Works Supply Co. in 1898 for tar traffic. The two tanks had a similar capacity, but they differed in both shape and dimensions. By 1919, the second, No. 141, was classified as a water tank, and by 1923 they were both being used to supply water to Medina Wharf. The height of the tank on No. 140 is believed to have been so arranged as to allow the steam crane boilers on the wharf to be filled by gravity following wash-out.

*A. B. MacLeod*

**Plate 155** By 1930, Medina Wharf had been rebuilt and the tanks were no longer required, so it was fortunate that they were both still on hand for conversion in 1932 into one of the country's first weed killing trains. For this purpose the tank of No. 443S was placed on the underframe of the IWR tar tank No. 61381, which was in its turn placed on the underframe of an LSWR covered goods wagon. There have been several photographs published recently of the two tanks as first converted, so we have chosen one that shows them in store at Ningwood about 1952, by which time they had acquired the two South Western underframes, one of which was mentioned above, following the withdrawal of Nos. 61381/2 in 1947. The length over headstocks was 18ft. and the wheelbase 10ft. 6in. Each tank was mounted centrally on its underframe. The dimensions of the nearer tank, No. 428S, were width 6ft. 4in., height 5ft. 9in., and length approximately 12ft. No. 443S was 6ft. 4in. x 5ft. 6in. x 13ft. 7in. They always ran with their laddered ends to the outside of the set, and although they had three-link couplings on their outer ends, they were coupled together by a screw coupling. In Southern days, they were painted red oxide; BR painted them black. Both were broken up in 1967.

*Authors' Collection*

**Plate 156** In 1911, the IWCR purchased 4 three plank dropside ballast wagons from the Midland Railway. These became Nos. 329-32, and here we see three of them being used to clear a chalk fall at St. Lawrence in March 1912. The Southern Railway recorded their dimensions as 13ft. 6in. x 7ft. 5in. x 1ft. 9in. However, we doubt the length, as MR ballast wagons were usually 14ft. 11in. long, and when the underframe of No. 329 was measured in 1963, that was its length.

*Lens of Sutton*

**Plate 157** Three of the IWCR ballast wagons were soon broken up by the Southern Railway, but No. 329 survived until 1970, having been rebuilt in 1932 with the body ironwork of ballast wagon No. 62894. The photograph was taken at Newport in June 1963 and shows No. DS62883 in this form, by which time its dimensions were 14ft. 11in. x 7ft. 8½in. x 2ft. 3in. The wheelbase was 8ft. 6in.

*A. Blackburn*

**Plate 158** In May 1912, the IWCR purchased this 5 ton travelling crane from the Midland Railway for the sum of £320, and the Central numbered it 'Crane No. 5'; the crane runner was wagon No. 28. The Southern renumbered them Nos. 429S and 429SM, and they have both survived to become part of the Isle of Wight's Steam Railway stock at Havenstreet. The crane carriage has a length of 14ft. 11in. and a width of 7ft. 6in. The wheelbase is 9ft. The runner is 14ft. 11in. x 7ft. 4½in. x 11in.; the wheelbase is 9ft.

*A. E. West*

## The Freshwater, Yarmouth & Newport Railway

This was very much a branch line, even by Isle of Wight standards, and the area it served certainly benefited from the railway's construction but no one ever made any money out of it. The railway was worked by the IWCR from its opening in 1899 until June 1913, after which the Freshwater Company worked the line themselves with a motley collection of rolling stock obtained from various sources. The goods wagons all came from the IWCR, and consisted of four covered goods wagons, twenty six open goods wagons, and a brake van. One presumes that the Central selected the vehicles which it sold, but if so, the open wagons were a very average collection, and they may have simply been twenty six empties most conveniently available. The four covered goods wagons were a definite group; they were four of the Central's five smallest vans and they may well have been selected as those most suited to the line's traffic. As for the brake van — who knows? It was in good order and the Central retained little better. Its IWCR number is not known, but it was probably either No. 1 or No. 4. Altogether it seems to have been a fair deal except that the Central did not make any cattle trucks available, and if there was one particular type of wagon the Freshwater needed, then it was cattle trucks, as nearly all the line's stations loaded cattle, and Yarmouth was the Island's main cattle port. To remedy this deficiency, the FY&NR converted five coal trucks into cattle wagons by simply fitting them with floor battens, two side rails and a corrugated-

iron roof. It all sounds a bit crude and, indeed, it was, but many hundreds of similar conversions were carried out on the mainland during World War I to carry Army horses, and that may be where the Company obtained the idea. The Southern were not short of cattle wagons in 1923, and quickly converted them back into open goods wagons.

The Freshwater Railway did not have a complete wagon numbering scheme; the coaching stock was numbered 1-12, and the goods brake van was No. 13. Thereafter, they started to renumber the wagons as and when they overhauled them. The covered goods wagons became Nos. 14-17, the cattle truck conversions were Nos. 18-22, and two other open wagons became Nos. 24 and 25. The remaining wagons retained their IWCR numbers, so from that one might guess that they did not require any major attention for over ten years. It has been recorded that the rolling stock was painted grey with white lettering. We have no reason to disbelieve this, as all the photographs we have seen certainly show a light colour. The stock was lettered 'FYN', but we do not know where the covered goods vans carried this lettering. However, on the open wagons the letters were painted on the middle of the left-hand quarter board, the letter 'F' being to the left of the diagonal strapping, and 'Y' and 'N' to the right. The number was in the corresponding position on the right-hand side of the wagon.

**Figure 52 & Plate 159** These show SR No. 438S, a former covered goods wagon that, we believe, was built at Newport in 1911 on the underframe of an old coal wagon. It was certainly one of four dimensionally similar vehicles which the IWCR sold to the Freshwater line in June 1913. The IWCR numbers are believed to have been 171-4, but this cannot be confirmed; they became FYN Nos. 14-7. FYN No. 15, the wagon drawn, became SR No. 47033 in March 1927. It was the last of the four to remain in service, and it was converted into a mess and tool van in August 1930. As such, it moved infrequently around the Island until April 1939, when it was grounded in Newport Yard for use as a tool store, and that is where one of the authors measured it in 1952.

*Authors' Collection*

END A                                    END B

S R
438S

TOOL VAN
ENGINEERS D⁰⁰
BRIDGE S⁰⁰ⁿ
TARE 4·10·0

3'·1" DIA. WHEELS.
8'·0"
13'·10½"
16'·10½"

7'·6"
END A
END B-OMIT WINDOW.

## FYNR 8 TON COVERED GOODS

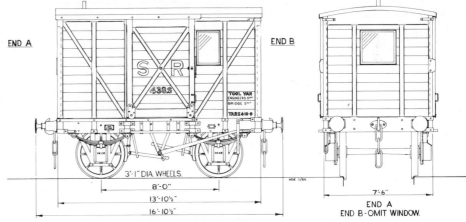

**Figure 53** In 1913, the FY&NR decided to work its own railway, and the IWCR sold them twenty six open and four covered goods wagons and one brake van. This is the brake van, which had formerly been purchased by the IWCR from the LBSCR. We know the Centràl had at least two, if not three, of these vehicles, but we cannot say if they were identical. This was possibly not the case, for this particular van is quite unlike any other Stroudley van we have seen in its detail work, and it is for this reason, plus the fact that our photograph of it in FY&NR livery is not suitable for reproduction, that we have drawn it. The Freshwater line used vacuum brakes on one of its two passenger train sets, and this van was provided with a vacuum through pipe, so presumably this was to allow for its use in a passenger train, when required. After withdrawal, the van body was grounded at St. Helen's, where it remained until very recently.

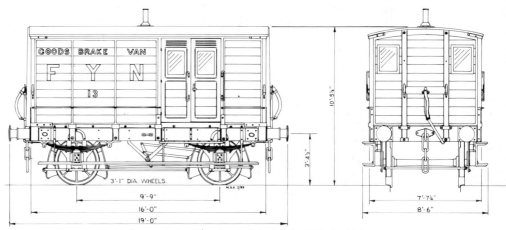

**FYNR (Ex-LBSCR) GOODS BRAKE VAN**

**Plate 160** In pre-Grouping days, the 'Terriers' handled most of the goods trains on the IWCR, whilst on the IWR the larger *Brading* or *Bonchurch* were the preferred engines. The 'Terriers' or the FY&NR Manning Wardle continued to be used on the Shide to Cement Mills chalk trains, on Medina Wharf, and on the minor branches, but elsewhere, from 1923, the Class 02s were used. Here we see No. W19 coming off the Newport line at Sandown in June 1928 with a short train that includes, as its last vehicle, what looks like the FY&NR Stroudley goods brake. Note that the screw coupling has been taken off the hook to make things easier for the shunters.

*H. F. Wheeller*

**Plate 161 (Right)** The Southern Railway found that one of the most pressing requirements it had to face in the Island was the urgent need to carry out a great deal of permanent way work, a task that was quite clearly going to take several years to complete. The Island could muster a reasonable number of bolsters and flat wagons, on which to carry the rails, but the IWCR only possessed four ballast wagons, and the IWR none at all. The Southern found its answer in a batch of very interesting 10 ton dropside wagons, which, whilst they were not classified as ballast wagons, had in fact been built as such for the firm of Price & Reeves, who, in 1899 had the contract to build the various spurs to connect the Chatham and South Eastern main lines at Chislehurst. On completion of this work the SECR took over fifty of these wagons and used them for general goods work up until World War I. In April 1917, most of them were sent to France for use by the ROD as ballast wagons. Their return to Britain was somewhat delayed after the war, and so it was that twenty of them were on hand at Ashford and could be made ready for service on the Island just when they were wanted. They were shipped to St. Helen's, one standing inside another, they proved to be ideal for the Island's ballast work, and in the course of time, Ryde replaced the original grease axleboxes with the LBSCR No. 7 oil box, which was used on most of the other Southern wagons on the Island. Two were damaged, and their ironwork was used to build new bodies on former IWCR wagons. Two others, which were the official replacements for the damaged wagons just mentioned, arrived in 1931. The whole class remained in use until 1966/7, and one, No. 62888, has survived to be preserved at Havenstreet. At the time of its withdrawal in 1981, it was the oldest wagon in use on the Southern Region. Another of these wagons, No. DS62895, is pictured here. **Figure 55** is a drawing of No. 62902, showing further detail variation.

*A. Blackburn*

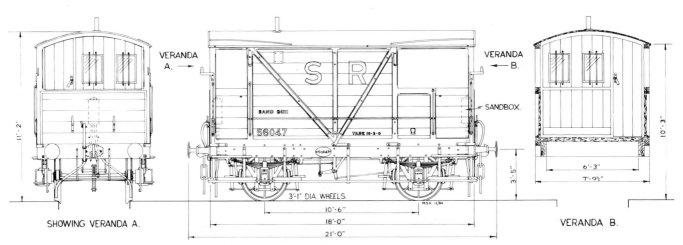

SHOWING VERANDA A.    VERANDA B.

**LSWR 10 TON GOODS BRAKE VAN** AS REBUILT
IN 1933 FROM DIAGRAM 1541 VEHICLES. A NEW DIAGRAM NUMBER
WAS NOT ALLOCATED.

## The Post-Grouping Scene

The first thing that the Southern Railway seems to have done about the wagons in the Isle of Wight was to send someone over from the mainland to measure them all up and, no doubt, write a report on his findings. There was an urgent requirement for twenty ED ballast wagons, and for twenty open goods wagons to replace those which were currently being broken up. Twenty former private owner ballast wagons were available at Ashford, and Lancing had twenty of its standard open goods ready. The latter were an obvious choice; they were suitable, there were outstanding orders for several hundred more, and by selecting an LBSCR type, they enabled the Southern Railway to rid itself of a large number of non-standard 6ft. 3in. wheel sets to somewhere where they would not cause any inconvenience. Both the LSWR and the SECR used either 6ft. 8in. or 6ft. 6in. wheels, the latter of course being the RCH/SR standard. With a potential requirement for large numbers of open goods wagons, it followed in the interest of standardisation that other Brighton types should be selected, and so they were, the only exceptions being four LSWR van trucks and the Diagram 1541 brake vans, also of LSWR origin, which the Southern seems to have selected as a standard type of brake to replace all the other types of old brake vans which it had inherited.

It might have been thought that the Southern would, with the benefits of standardisation, have been able to reduce the size of the wagon fleet on the Island, but Waterloo was more concerned with reducing the Island's workshop costs, and the size of the fleet actually increased somewhat.

The Southern reconstructed the dock facilities at both St. Helen's and Medina, and the general goods traffic was now concentrated at St. Helen's, with coal and other minerals, such as roadstone, at Medina. Here massive storage pens were constructed with the object of relieving the wagon supply problems previously mentioned. These must have helped the situation, but they never cured it, probably because the new wharf could handle larger colliers, which in their turn required more trucks. In Southern days, Medina handled about 100,000 tons of coal annually, most of which was household coal, destined for every station in the Island with a siding. In addition to this, there were large quantities of 'gas coal' for the gasworks at Newport, Ryde and Shanklin, plus of course the 'loco coal' for Newport and Ryde.

In 1936, the Southern decided to transfer all the general goods traffic to Messrs Pickford's wharf at Cowes for onward delivery by road; they were a railway-owned company, and it made good sense. Henceforth, St. Helen's would handle only departmental traffic and track ballast which was obtained by dredging the approaches to the harbour. This left half the covered goods and van trucks spare, and some of the latter were broken up as surplus to requirements, but the vans lay about at St. Helen's until they were returned to the mainland after the war for use as stores vans. The aftermath of the war found the open wagon fleet in a very run down condition, and it was decided to send over some SR steel-framed 13 ton open wagons in replacement for an equivalent tonnage of Brighton five planks, which were then broken up. Meanwhile, it had been decided to give up using the sea ballast in favour of Blackwater gravel. It was thought that the LBSCR 20 ton ballast hoppers would be a more suitable and modern replacement for the old EDs to carry this stone, and ten were sent over in 1947. Unfortunately, they suffered extensively from corrosion, and it was not long before the EDs were again being used. The stock figure for 31st December 1948 in **Table A** shows what might be called the 'modernised' post-war fleet position, and this remained more or less intact until large scale withdrawals started following the line and gasworks closures of the early 1950s.

**Plate 162 (Above Right)** The ironwork of wagon No. 62889 as mounted on the underframe of open goods wagon No. 28181/IWCR No. 161. The dimensions were, length 14ft. 11⅜, width 7ft. 4¼ in., wheelbase 8ft. 6in.

*A. Blackburn*

**Figure 54 (Left)** In 1933, four Diagram 1541 brake vans of LSWR origin were rebuilt at Ryde with a second balcony and sand gear for use with the 40-wagon coal trains, made possible by the arrival of the Class E1 engines. Note the Westinghouse pipe provided. It is thought that this was for use on the Freshwater line mail trains. Their numbers were 56044/6-8.

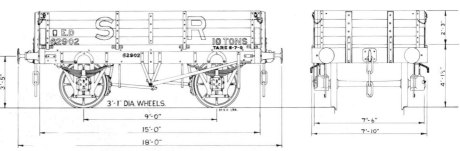

**SECR 10 TON DROPSIDE OPEN GOODS**
AS REBUILT WITH LBSCR FITTINGS FOR I.O.W. BALLAST/E.D. SERVICE.
NOMINALLY S.R. DIAGRAM 1352.

**Figure 55 ▶**

**Plate 163** In May 1947, two Adams tenders, taken from withdrawn A12 class locomotives, were transferred to the Island to replace the two IWR tar tanks, Nos. 61384/5. They saw little, if any service before being returned to the mainland in November 1950. They were given the Diagram number 1716. Their length over buffers was 22ft. 9½ in., over buffer beams 19ft. 10½ in. The width over tank sides was 7ft. 6in., the wheels were 3ft. 9¾ in. in diameter, and the wheelbase was 6ft. 6in. + 6ft. 6in. The inscription on the side reads 'not to be coupled to vehicles of the same type or next to engines'; clearly the Civil Engineer did not like them.

*A. E. West*

**Plate 164** One of the 88 SR eight plank open goods wagons to Diagram 1379, which were sent to the Island during 1948/9 as a replacement for approximately 115 of the Brighton five planks which were withdrawn at this time. The fact that the first of these Eastleigh-designed wagons was built in the same year as the last of Diagram 1364 underlines just how dated Lancing's construction had become by 1926. Diagram 1379 will be dealt with in detail in **Volume Four**. Their dimensions were 17ft. 6in. x 7ft. 11in. x 4ft. 7⅜ in. and the wheelbase was 9ft.

*A. Blackburn*

**Plate 165** Whilst neither the IWR or the IWCR possessed the resources to produce all the components for a new wagon, both Ryde and Newport were well able to carry out extensive work using materials purchased from outside suppliers. Ryde, for instance, purchased so much of its timber ready prepared from G. Wheeler & Co., a local builder, that the records actually credited this company as having built the wagons. This very interesting photograph shows a Brighton five plank wagon being repaired by Ryde Works in the early 1960s, and well illustrates the scale of the work undertaken. The far side solebar and a headstock are out, as are the middle longitudinals. The crib rail is on the ground, and it is worth noting that No. 64392 was one of the very few Brighton open wagons in the Island with single 'vee' hangers. Unfortunately its earlier SR number is not known. *A. Blackburn*

**Plate 166** This interesting photograph, taken at Newport in September 1953, does not show a resurgence of cattle traffic in BR days, but sadly the Island's last three cattle trucks and horse-box en route from Yarmouth to St. Helen's prior to the closure of the Freshwater line. Two years later, they would make just one more journey to Ryde for breaking up. Note the former 'Freshwater' covered goods wagon as a grounded body on the extreme right.

*Authors' Collection*

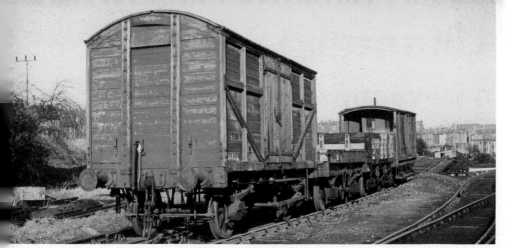

**Plate 167** In 1967, one of the authors, together with fellow railwaymen, managed to get four of the Island's wagons back from the Island for inclusion in the National Collection of preserved vehicles. Here we see these wagons waiting to leave Ryde. From the far end they are goods brake van No. 56055/ LSWR No. 99 of 1894, open wagon No. 27884/ LBSCR No. 3537 of 1912, van truck No. 60562/ LSWR No. 5830 of 1898, and lastly former cattle truck No. 46924/LBSCR No. 4047 of 1922.

*A. Blackburn*

### TABLE A — Wagon totals by type as at 31st December 1922, 1932, 1947 and 1948

| Type | 31/12/22 IWR | IWC | FYN | Totals | 31/12/32 SR | 31/12/47 SR | 31/12/48 BR |
|---|---|---|---|---|---|---|---|
| **Revenue** | | | | | | | |
| Open Goods | 189 | 251 | 22 | 462 | 459 | 455 | 459 |
| Covered Goods | 12 | 45 | 4 | 61 | 48 | 42 | 21 |
| Cattle Wagons | 3 | 8 | 4 | 15 | 7 | 3 | 3 |
| Goods Brake Vans | 2 | 3 | 1 | 6 | 13 | 12 | 12 |
| Timber Trucks | 5 | 6 | - | 11 | 20 | 20 | 20 |
| Flat Trucks | 8 | 3 | - | 11 | 23 | 14 | 14 |
| Tar Tanks | 2 | 1 | - | 3 | 2 | 2 | 2 |
| *Totals* | 221 | 317 | 31 | 569 | 572 | 548 | 531 |
| **Departmental** | | | | | | | |
| Ballast Wagons | - | 4 | - | 4 | 20 | 30 | 30 |
| Travelling Cranes | 2 | 1 | - | 3 | 3 | 3 | 3 |
| Match Trucks | 1 | 1 | - | 2 | 2 | 2 | 2 |
| Mess and Tool Vans | - | - | - | - | 4 | 8 | 8 |
| Loco. Coal Wagons | - | - | - | - | 12 | 12 | 12 |
| Departmental Brake Vans | - | - | - | - | 1 | 1 | 1 |
| Water Tanks | - | 2 | - | 2 | 2 | 2 | 2 |
| Boiler Trolleys | - | - | - | - | 1 | 1 | 1 |
| Yard Wagons | - | - | - | - | 1 | 1 | 1 |
| Stores Vans | - | - | - | - | - | 3 | 5 |
| Dock Wagons | - | - | - | - | - | 1 | 1 |
| *Totals* | 3 | 8 | 0 | 11 | 46 | 64 | 66 |
| *GRAND TOTALS* | 224 | 325 | 31 | 580 | 618 | 612 | 597 |

Of the 'Revenue' stock extant at 31/12/32, all were SR importations except for nine open goods wagons, one cattle truck, one goods brake van and the two tar tanks. Of the 'Departmentals' on the same date, however, all were ex-Island companies' stock except for eighteen of the ballast wagons.

### TABLE B — SR-BR Transfers to Isle of Wight 1924-49 (No wagon transfers in 1933/5/6/40-6)

| Type | Origin | Diagram | 1924 | 25 | 26 | 27 | 28 | 29 | 30 | 31 | 32 | 34 | 37 | 38 | 39 | 47 | 48 | 49 | Totals |
|---|---|---|---|---|---|---|---|---|---|---|---|---|---|---|---|---|---|---|---|
| Open Goods | LBSCR | 1369 | 20 | 6 | 50 | 68 | 70 | 75 | 75 | 86 | - | - | 1 | - | - | 6 | - | - | 457 |
| Open Goods | SR | 1379 | - | - | - | - | - | - | - | - | - | - | - | - | - | - | 48 | 40 | 88 |
| Mineral | SR Rebuild | 1374 | - | - | - | - | - | - | - | - | 1 | - | - | - | - | - | - | - | 1 |
| Covered Goods | LBSCR | 1433 | - | - | - | - | - | 8 | - | - | - | - | - | - | - | - | - | - | 8 |
| Covered Goods | LBSCR | 1434 | - | - | - | - | - | - | 5 | 8 | - | - | - | - | - | - | - | - | 13 |
| Covered Goods | LBSCR | 1436 | - | - | - | 12 | 7 | 7 | 1 | - | - | - | - | 1 | - | - | - | - | 28 |
| Cattle Trucks | LBSCR | 1527/8 | - | - | - | 3 | 1 | 2 | - | - | - | - | - | - | - | - | - | - | 6 |
| Brake Vans | LSWR | 1541 | - | 1 | - | 2 | 3 | - | 1 | 2 | 3 | - | - | 2 | - | - | - | - | 14 |
| Brake Vans | LSWR | 1542 | - | - | - | - | - | - | - | - | - | - | - | - | - | - | 1 | - | 1 |
| Single Bolsters | LBSCR | 1616 | - | - | - | - | 10 | - | 5 | - | - | - | - | - | - | - | - | - | 15 |
| Single Bolsters | LBSCR | 1617 | - | - | - | - | 5 | - | - | - | - | - | - | - | - | - | - | - | 5 |
| Van Trucks | LSWR | 1641 | - | - | - | 4 | - | - | - | - | - | - | - | - | - | - | - | - | 4 |
| Van Trucks | LBSCR | 1661 | - | - | - | - | 12 | 4 | 3 | - | - | - | - | - | - | - | - | - | 19 |
| Tar Tanks | SR Rebuild | 1716 | - | - | - | - | - | - | - | - | - | - | - | - | - | 2 | - | - | 2 |
| Ballast Wagons | PO/SECR | 1352 | 18 | - | - | - | - | - | 2 | - | - | - | - | - | - | - | - | - | 20 |
| Ballast Wagons | LBSCR | 1751 | - | - | - | 18 | - | - | - | - | - | - | - | - | - | - | - | - | 18 |
| Ballast Wagons | LBSCR | 1755 | - | - | - | - | - | - | - | - | - | - | - | - | - | 10 | - | - | 10 |
| *Totals* | | | 38 | 7 | 50 | 107 | 108 | 96 | 92 | 96 | 3 | 1 | 1 | 2 | 1 | 18 | 49 | 40 | 709 |

*Notes:* The 76 open goods wagons transferred in the period 1924-6 were new; all the other vehicles transferred were previously used on the mainland.

The one wagon transferred in 1937 was a loco. coal wagon.

The one wagon transferred in 1939 was a mess and tool van.

The two brake vans transferred in 1938 were of 15 tons, all the other Diagram 1541 brake vans were 10 tons.

Four of the Diagram 1617 and five of the Diagram 1616 wagons (Nos. 59033-41), transferred in 1928, were for the use of the Engineer's Dept. and were painted in red oxide livery, the remainder were brown.

The 18 dumb-buffered ballast wagons transferred in 1927 were for use on the various SR improvement schemes carried out between 1927 and 1930, after which they were broken up.

# Chapter 12
# The Plymouth, Devonport & South Western Junction Railway

Before discussing the wagons owned by the PD&SWJR, it should perhaps be explained that this Company's main line from Lidford to Devonport was leased to and operated by the LSWR from the date of its opening in 1890. The rolling stock with which we are concerned was required for a branch of the railway from Bere Alston to Callington, this section of the line not being opened until 1908. The line had its origins in the East Cornwall Mineral Railway, a 3ft. 6in. gauge line opened in 1872 connecting the mines and quarries in the area with a quay on the River Tamar at Calstock. The PD&SWJR purchased this line in 1894, and eventually rebuilt and extended it across the River Tamar to Bere Alston as a passenger-carrying standard gauge light railway.

H. F. Stephens, the well-known light railway engineer, was in charge of the line's reconstruction. With gradients as steep as 1 in 38, he very wisely ordered new and powerful locomotives, but most of the remaining stock was purchased second-hand. The passenger vehicles came from the LSWR but for his goods wagons Stephens went to R. Y. Pickering of Wishaw, near Glasgow, a firm much favoured by him at the time. They arranged to supply fifty open and two covered goods wagons, purchased second-hand from the Midland Railway at Derby. Second-hand brake vans were also considered but, mindful perhaps of the gradients, it was eventually decided that Pickering should build two new vans, which they did to their general arrangement drawing, No. 4439.

The open wagons consisted of two classes, both of which, from photographs and dimensions, can be confirmed as standard 8 ton Midland Railway designs. The first group comprised 30 three plank dropsides, and the second 20 five plank open wagons. From Pickering's records we know that these open wagons were numbered from 1 to 50, and from the evidence of three photographs, and a Southern Railway internal wagons stock list, it is believed that the dropsides were Nos. 1-30 and the five planks Nos. 31-50, but this is not definite. The two covered goods wagons were numbered 51 and 52, in all probability being standard MR vehicles of the well-known offset sliding door type, but neither photographs or dimensions have been found to confirm this. **Figure 46** on **page 84** illustrates what were probably similar vehicles purchased by the Isle of Wight Central Railway.

The brake vans were numbered 53 and 54, and were rather unusual on several counts. The very practical arrangement of the handbrake is noteworthy, as is the recessing of the internal partition to suit. The provision of vacuum brakes on a goods brake van was unusual at this period, especially as none of the other goods stock was so equipped. Two possible reasons for this come to mind; namely the working of vacuum-braked LSWR van trains conveying market produce as was common in later years, or the working of mixed trains with the possibility that these travelled towards Calstock with the brake van next to the passenger vehicles, so as to increase the amount of brake power under the control of the driver, rather than in the conventional position at the rear of the train. As the gradient fell in both directions towards Calstock any breakaway would be kept in check by the rest of the train. Such mixed trains travelling away from Calstock would of course have to be marshalled in the normal manner with the brake van as the last vehicle. The very low buffer height on these vans seems to have come about as a result of Stephens requiring that the wheels and axles be the same as those fitted under the MR wagons; presumably it had originally been intended to fit wheels of a larger diameter.

The wagon stock livery was recorded by R. Y. Pickering as 'bright red (same as (William) Cory's)'. Ironwork was black with lettering and numbers in white, shaded black on the wagons, but the brake vans received unshaded letters despite instructions to the contrary. It is worth noting, however, that this same instruction stated that the lettering was to have been 'PD&SWJ', but in practice the 'J' was omitted.

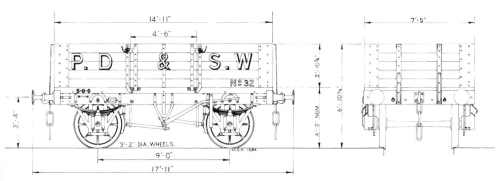

PD&SWJR 5 PLANK OPEN GOODS
EX-MIDLAND RAILWAY VEHICLES.

**Figure 56** The five plank open goods wagon.

**Plate 168** Five plank open wagons, Nos. 32 and 35, at Callington before 1923. The only visible modifications are the provision of a centre strap on the doors and metal door stops mounted on the solebars. Note that the door straps have been added since the wagons were lettered. The numbers and tare weights appear to be unshaded.
*Authors' Collection*

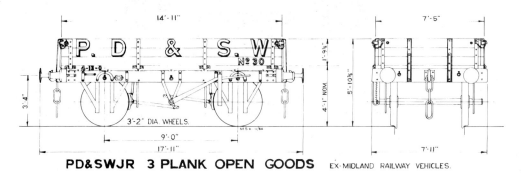

PD&SWJR 3 PLANK OPEN GOODS EX-MIDLAND RAILWAY VEHICLES.

**Figure 57**  The three plank dropside wagon.

The proportionally large number of open wagons reflected the line's origins (the ECMR owned 2 engines, 26 open wagons, 16 covered wagons, 2 service and 3 brake vehicles) but in fact the local mining activity was already nearing its end by the time the line was rebuilt. It had been intended that the mineral traffic should continue to be worked down to Calstock Quay by way of a wagon lift, but coastal shipping was also on the wane, and it would seem that the lift saw little use between 1908, and when it finally closed in 1934. One wonders if the PD&SWJR goods stock was confined to the line. The rolling stock of the minor railways was excluded from the common-user policies of World War I, and it seems that most of the railways' wagons were in hand when the LSWR took over the line in 1922. We say 'most' because one of the covered goods wagons was scrapped before June 1917 and the other failed to receive an LSWR number. Of the open wagons, seven did not have LSWR numbers allocated and the rest became Nos. 01 to 043 in one of the LSWR's internal user lists. Despite the fact that they agreed with two diagrams issued to cover the similar S&DJR wagons, none received diagram numbers. Later, the remaining survivors became Nos. 0238s to 0263s in the Southern Railway service stock fleet, mainly at Eastleigh Works, but at least one example roamed as far afield as Feltham.

The brake vans were recorded in the LSWR diagram book but do not seem to have had LSWR numbers allocated. The SR gave them numbers 56042/3, both being renumbered at Eastleigh in November 1925. It is thought they both remained on the Callington branch until scrapped, No. 56043 (ex-No. 54) lasting until September 1928, and its running mate until March 1930.

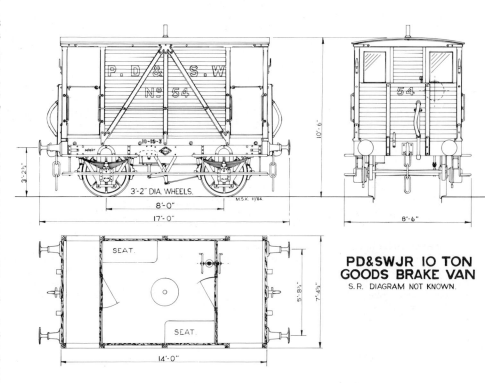

PD&SWJR 10 TON
GOODS BRAKE VAN
S.R. DIAGRAM NOT KNOWN.

**Figure 58**  The PD&SWJR brake van.

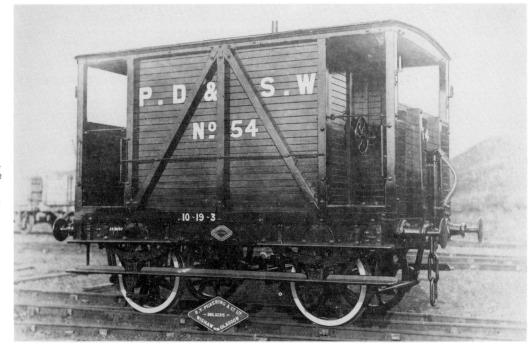

**Plate 169**  The makers' photograph of No. 54, as completed in October 1907. The excellent standard of finish will be noted.
*R. Y. Pickering Ltd.*

# Chapter 13
## The Lynton & Barnstaple Railway

This unique 1ft. 11½in. gauge railway forms part of our story by virtue of the fact that it became Southern Railway property at the Grouping. The line's history and final demise have been well documented already, with at least three of the previously published accounts including details of the rolling stock. The authors are unable to add a great deal to these, but all three histories contain certain discrepancies and it is fair to state that the official records compiled by the Southern Railway include several more. Many of the latter are obvious in nature and are relatively easily identified. In absence, therefore, of any totally reliable source of information, the authors have taken the official records as the most accurate, modifying them where photographic and other evidence suggests otherwise.

The Southern Railway took the trouble to record details of the rolling stock, entering these into the registers in precisely the same format as the standard gauge stock, producing diagrams for each design in addition. By good fortune, the general arrangement drawings of the wagons ordered by the Southern Railway in 1927 have survived, enabling these details to supplement those on the diagrams. In the case of the 1927 wagons, the diagrams and general arrangement drawings are in good agreement.

The original goods rolling stock was ordered from the Bristol Wagon & Carriage Company in 1897 and comprised eight open and six covered goods vehicles, each running on four wheels, plus two bogie open wagons and two bogie goods brake vans. The bogie vehicles were clearly found to be more suitable since all subsequent additions were of this type. Six more wagons were added to stock between 1900 and 1913, whilst another eight, and two cranes, were provided by the Southern Railway. All survived until the line closed on 29th September 1935, being officially condemned in the following month, and auctioned in lots along with all the other equipment in November 1935. Subsequently, most of the steel underframes accompanied the last surviving locomotive to a coffee plantation in Brazil in 1936. A summary of the goods rolling stock, with relevant details, is as follows.

| SR Diagram | SR Numbers | L&BR Numbers | Capacity (Tons) | Vehicle Type | Underframe Type | Brake Gear | Built by | Date Built |
|---|---|---|---|---|---|---|---|---|
| 1391 | 28313 (28265) | 22 | 8 | Bogie Open Goods | Timber | VP | Bristol W&C Co. | 1903 |
| 1392 | 28312 (28261) | 19 | 6 | Bogie Open Goods | Steel | VP | Rebuilt L&BR | 1900 |
| 1393 | 28301/2 (28262/3) | 12, 13 | 8 | Bogie Open Goods | Steel | V | Bristol W&C Co. | 1897 |
| 1394 | 28304-11 (28253-60) | 1, 2, 8-11, 17, 18 | 4 | Open Goods | Steel | V | Bristol W&C Co. | 1897 |
| 1395 | 28303 (28264) | 24 | 8 | Bogie Open Goods | Steel | V | L&BR Pilton Works | 1913 |
| 1396 | 28316-9 | - | 8 | Bogie Open Goods | Steel | V | J&F Howard & Co. | 1927 |
| 1397 | 28314/5 (28266/7) | 20, 21 | 8 | Bogie Platform | Timber | V | Bristol W&C Co. | 1902 |
| 1453 | 47036-41 | 3, 4, 6, 7, 15, 16 | 4 | Covered Goods | Steel | V | Bristol W&C Co. | 1897 |
| 1456 | 47042-5 | - | 8 | Bogie Covered Goods | Steel | V | J&F Howard & Co. | 1927 |
| 1589 | 56041 | 23 | 8 | Bogie Goods Brake | Timber | V | L&BR Pilton Works | 1908 |
| 1590 | 56039/40 | 5, 14 | 8 | Bogie Goods Brake | Steel | V | Bristol W&C Co. | 1897 |
| - | 441s, 442s | - | 3/4½ | Travelling Crane | Steel | - | Chambers Scott & Co. | See Note 3 |
| - | 441sm | - | - | Match Truck | Steel | - | SR Lancing Works | 1927 |

*Notes:*
1. Open goods wagon numbers in brackets refer to those originally allocated early in 1923. Only the numbers 28255/60 appear to have been carried by the vehicles concerned.
2. When built, the 1897 open and covered goods wagons were devoid of handbrake levers, but one was later provided on one side only. Goods brake vans had internal screw brake levers. Most other L&BR wagons had a brake lever on one side only, and the 1927 open wagons and covered goods vehicles were the only ones to have a lever on both sides.
3. Cranes Nos. 441s and 442s were purchased from George Cohen & Sons in 1926 and, almost certainly, were ex-War Department. They could lift 3 tons at 15ft. radius or 4½ tons at 11ft. 6in. radius. The SR service stock register gives their dimensions as 11ft. 3in. long, and 6ft. 8½in. wide. No. 441s was coupled to match truck No. 441sm, and was based at the Company's headquarters/workshops at Pilton Yard, Barnstaple. No. 442s was used in Lynton goods yard, mounted on a short section of isolated track as a static crane.

L&BR livery was light grey with black ironwork and running gear. All lettering was white, the capacity and tare weight inscriptions usually being in italic script, however block lettering was sometimes used instead. After the Grouping, several wagons appeared in a hybrid L&BR/SR brown livery, retaining their L&BR numbers but lettered 'SR', often in a very unorthodox style. A typical example was wagon No. 22, as depicted in **Figure 61**. By about 1929, all wagons carried standard Southern Railway brown livery with white lettering.

All bogie open wagons were used for carrying ballast, and to prevent overloading the Southern Railway added metal strips bolted internally along the sides and ends to indicate the loading limit. The position of these varied from diagram to diagram and they were painted red to make them more conspicuous. A stencilled instruction was carried on the sides drawing attention to this, but the lettering was so small that it cannot be deciphered in any known photographs.

**Plate 170** Four-wheeled open wagon No. 10, as delivered in 1898 with top-hung doors, safety chains at each end and no handbrake lever. Other features to note are the steel under-frame, vacuum brakes and Norwegian-style centre buffer/couplings. The tare weight of 2 tons 7 cwt. 3 qtr. was typical until the vehicles were widened, and pairs of side-hung doors, tarpaulin sheet rail and a brake lever were added. The original lettering layout should also be noted.

*North Devon Athenaeum*

**Plate 171** Diagram 1394, open wagon No. 9, later SR No. 28307, photographed at Lynton. This shows the condition in which all the four-wheeled open wagons were running by 1907, with side-hung doors, sheet rail and floor plank-ing extending through the side planks. The position of the Company initials should be com-pared with No. 10 above. Yet another lettering variation appears below in **Figure 59**.

*L&GRP*

**Figure 59** A drawing of the original four wheeled goods stock.

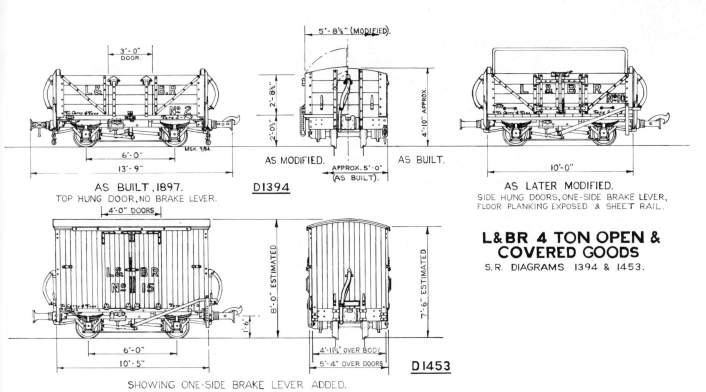

AS BUILT, 1897.
TOP HUNG DOOR, NO BRAKE LEVER.

D1394

AS LATER MODIFIED.
SIDE HUNG DOORS, ONE-SIDE BRAKE LEVER,
FLOOR PLANKING EXPOSED & SHEET RAIL.

D1453

SHOWING ONE-SIDE BRAKE LEVER ADDED.

## L&BR 4 TON OPEN & COVERED GOODS
S.R. DIAGRAMS 1394 & 1453.

**Plate 172** Wagon No. 28308, formerly L&BR No. 10, as running-in 1935. Compare the details of the door hinges with No. 9. Clearly No. 9 reused the old ironwork whereas No. 10 had new castings made. Several other small detail differences may be spotted amongst the eight examples of this diagram. It was these vehicles which were likened to a 'child's wheelbarrow' by a Lynton councillor when closure of the line was first announced by the Southern Railway in the spring of 1935.

*A. B. Macleod*

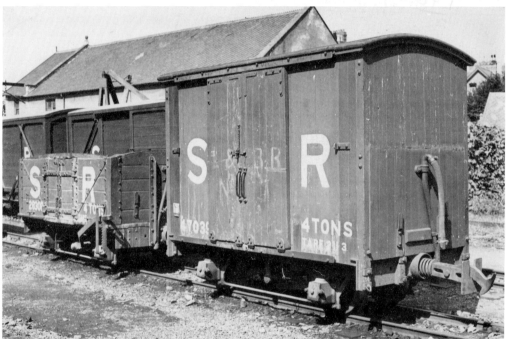

**Plate 173** Unlike the open wagons, the four-wheeled vans remained almost unaltered throughout, save for the addition of a brake lever on one side, not visible in this 1935 view at Pilton Yard. SR No. 47039, formerly L&BR No. 7, awaits its next duty in company with open wagon No. 28308. Notice that the pre-Grouping lettering is visible under the coat of SR brown.

*J. G. Dewing*

Several types of bogie open wagon were built for the line between 1897 and 1913. **Figure 60 (opposite)** illustrates the original 1897 design to Diagram 1393, an odd wagon acquired in 1900 to Diagram 1392, and the last wagon to be added to stock before the Grouping, to Diagram 1395. The Southern Railway allocation of diagram numbers is inexplicable, since they do not run in ascending order of capacity, as one might expect. The same may be said of the running numbers. Wagon No. 28303 appears in **Plate 180** on **page 102**. The vehicle placed in traffic in 1900 is something of a mystery and has previously been credited to the contractor responsible for the line's construction. This theory seems quite plausible since the L&BR was thenattempting to dispose of the contractor's other effects, following bankruptcy. Little success appears to have been acheived, since photographs of the 1930s show several of the tipper wagons used by the contractor still littering Pilton Yard and other places along the line. Wagon No. 28312 was shorter, narrower, and of smaller capacity

than any of the others, whilst its underframe and bogies were radically different. The bodywork was, however, standard with all the other bogie open wagons built up to 1913, so it would appear that the L&BR did at least construct this, which is exactly how the SR registers record the details. Unfortunately, it has not proved possible to locate any good photographs, so the details of brake gear cannot be incorporated on the drawing. However it is known that a screw brake was fitted originally.

The 1897 bogie open wagons saw several modifications during their working lives, in addition to the fitting of a brake lever. By 1906 they had two pairs of 3-part doors (i.e. side-hung top doors with a drop flap below) on each side, and a few years later received a single pair of side-hung doors, offset to the left, on each side. This later rebuilding was quite extensive and involved repositioning of much of the side strapping.

**Plate 175** A comparison between four-wheeled open wagon No. 18 and bogie open wagon No. 13 at Woody Bay, probably dating from about 1920. Both vehicles are in their finally modified state. Although the original bogie open wagons received several modifications, the later vehicles do not appear to have been reconstructed in any way.
*L&GRP*

**Figure 60**

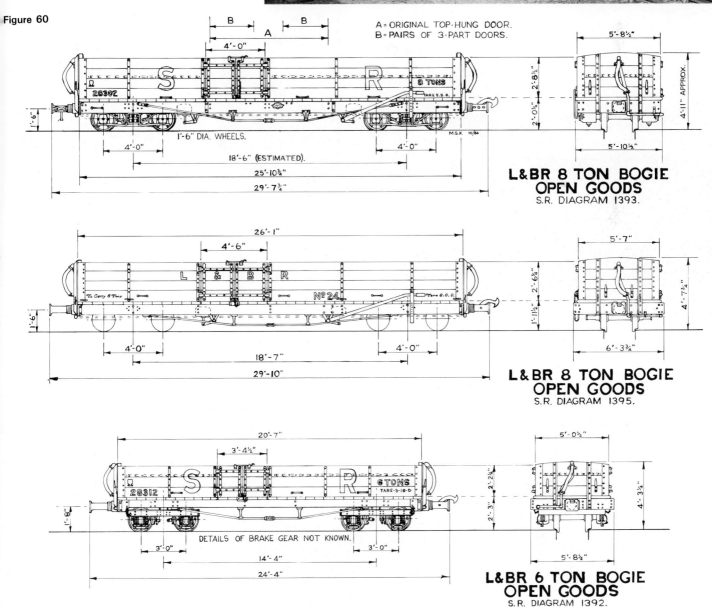

A = ORIGINAL TOP-HUNG DOOR.
B = PAIRS OF 3-PART DOORS.

**L&BR 8 TON BOGIE OPEN GOODS**
S.R. DIAGRAM 1393.

**L&BR 8 TON BOGIE OPEN GOODS**
S.R. DIAGRAM 1395.

**L&BR 6 TON BOGIE OPEN GOODS**
S.R. DIAGRAM 1392.

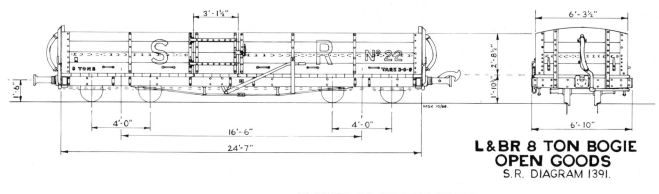

**L&BR 8 TON BOGIE
OPEN GOODS**
S.R. DIAGRAM 1391.

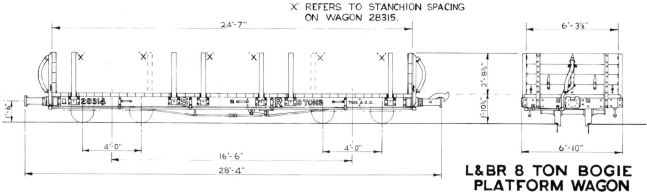

'X' REFERS TO STANCHION SPACING
ON WAGON 28315.

**L&BR 8 TON BOGIE
PLATFORM WAGON**
S.R. DIAGRAM 1397.

The Company soon found it had underestimated the amount of goods stock required but was not in a position to purchase more until 1902. Three wagons were ordered from Bristol Wagon & Carriage Company in that year, the last such order placed with that Company by the L&BR. One vehicle, a bogie open wagon, was not delivered until the following year and was unique in having only one side-hung door on each side. All three had timber underframes, unlike the 1897 vehicles, and are illustrated above in **Figure 61**.

**Plate 176** This shows one of the two bogie flat wagons, an entirely new design which fulfilled the requirement for carrying bulky loads. The eight stanchions were removable, there being twelve possible mounting positions for them. By SR days, each wagon had a different stanchion spacing, but it is not known if this was a feature when delivered in 1902. No. 28314 was photographed at Pilton Yard in 1935.

*A. B. Macleod*

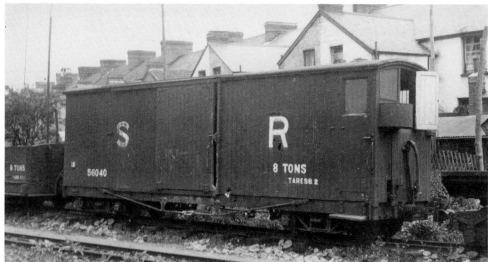

**Plate 177** The two original brake vans were also bogie vehicles, equipped with sliding doors and, when built, an open veranda and dog box, as drawn in **Figure 62 (Right)**. These details were altered by about 1908, in which form No. 56040 was photographed in 1935.

*Authors' Collection*

**Plate 178 (Left)** In 1908, the Company added a further brake van to stock, No. 23 in the fleet. Unlike the originals, this was built at Pilton, the works plate reading 'L&BR CO. PILTON BRIDGE BARNSTAPLE'. It had a timber underframe and was equipped with guards' look-outs at one end. As with the other brake vans, oil lighting was fitted.

*North Devon Athenaeum*

**Plate 179 (Right)** The same van in Southern Railway livery, berthed in the short siding adjacent to Chelfham Viaduct on 17th August 1935. This vehicle remained unaltered throughout its working life and was often used to carry passengers' luggage and small parcels in just the same manner as the LSWR 'Road' brake vans. Pure goods trains were unusual on the line, the normal mode of operation being by mixed train. Just whether the goods wagons were marshalled at the front or rear of the train depended on their destination, but once steam heating was provided they had to be coupled at the rear of the train in winter.

*H. F. Wheeller*

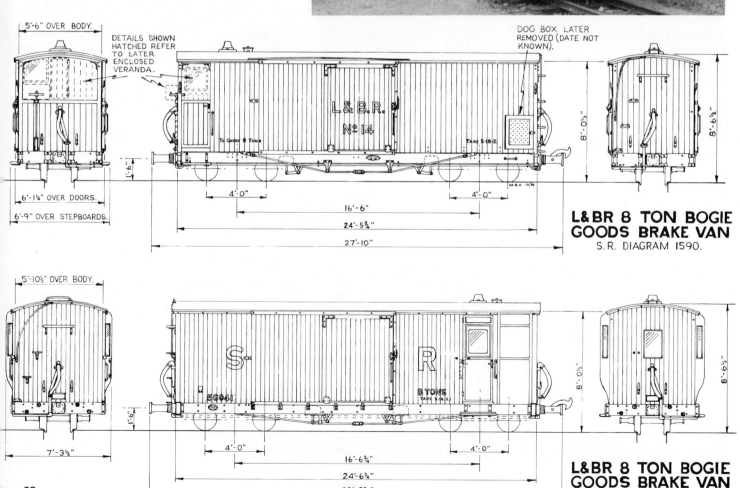

**L&BR 8 TON BOGIE GOODS BRAKE VAN**
S.R. DIAGRAM 1590.

**L&BR 8 TON BOGIE GOODS BRAKE VAN**
S.R. DIAGRAM 1589.

Figure 62

**Plate 180** In view of the diminishing traffic returns, it is perhaps surprising that the Southern found it necessary to provide additional goods rolling stock. Amongst these were two cranes, Nos. 441s and 442s in the service stock list. The latter is seen in this view, in static use at Lynton goods yard on 17th August 1935, together with 1913-built open wagon No. 28303. It is unlikely that either crane saw much use during their nine year sojourn on the line.

*H. F. Wheeller*

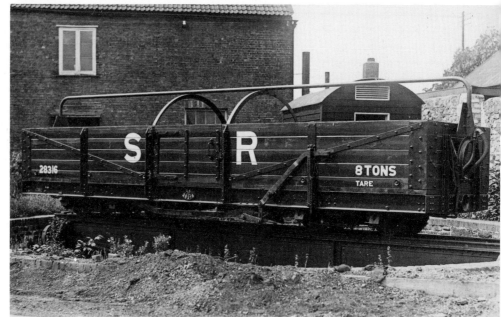

**Plate 181** Four bogie open wagons and four bogie vans were ordered from J. & F. Howard of Bedford, these being delivered in August 1927. This view illustrates No. 28316, the first of the open wagons, on the turntable at Pilton when new, and before couplings had been fitted. Note also that the tare weight has yet to be painted on. These were the only bogie open wagons to have centrally-positioned doors and sheet rails. They remained unmodified for the whole of their short working lives.

*British Rail*

**Plate 182** The four bogie vans being delivered at Barnstaple Town in August 1927. This shows the original design with timber cross-bracing, somewhat reminiscent of LSWR vans. After a few years in service, the bodywork showed signs of distortion, and all four had to be rebuilt (as illustrated on the next page). The reconstruction was fairly extensive and included substitution of the timber bracing by steel channels and plates. The roof timbers and body framing at the ends were also modified and strengthened.

*British Rail*

**Plate 183** Covered goods wagon No. 47044 on Pilton turntable in May 1935, showing the final appearance of these vans. It is probably true to state that these were the most heavily used of the goods vehicles after 1927. The date of rebuilding is not certain, and might have taken place at any time between 1929 and 1933.

*H. C. Casserley*

**Figure 63** A drawing of the 1927 open wagons and vans.

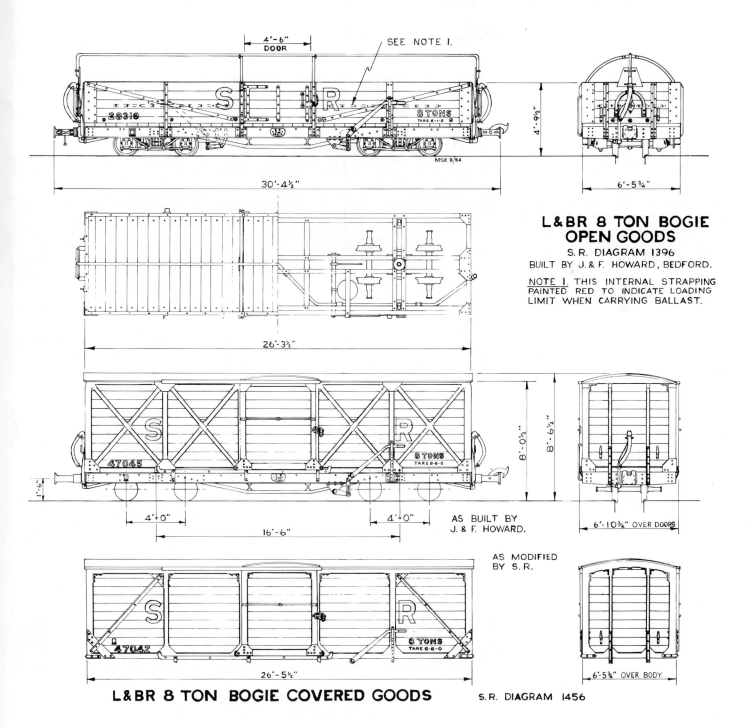

SEE NOTE I.

4'-6"
DOOR

4'-9½"

28319   8 TONS
TARE 6-1-0

MSK 8/84

30'-4½"

6'-5¾"

## L&BR 8 TON BOGIE OPEN GOODS
S.R. DIAGRAM 1396
BUILT BY J. & F. HOWARD, BEDFORD.

NOTE I. THIS INTERNAL STRAPPING PAINTED RED TO INDICATE LOADING LIMIT WHEN CARRYING BALLAST.

26'-3½"

47045   8 TONS
TARE 6-6-0

8'-0½"   8'-6½"

1'-6"

4'-0"   4'-0"

16'-6"

AS BUILT BY
J. & F. HOWARD.

6'-10¾" OVER DOORS

AS MODIFIED
BY S.R.

47042   8 TONS
TARE 6-6-0

26'-5½"

6'-5¾" OVER BODY.

## L&BR 8 TON BOGIE COVERED GOODS
S.R. DIAGRAM 1456

# Appendix 1
## Southern Railway Diagram and Running Numbers

Note: Numbering details given are those allocated from 1923. Not all pre-Grouping wagons actually received their new numbers before being scrapped. The renumbering scheme took some time to implement and wagons could still be seen in pre-Grouping livery until the mid-1930s. Occasional examples still existed as late as 1939.

| SR Diagram | Origin | Vehicle Type | Capacity (tons) | Average Tare | SR Running Numbers | Total | Notes | Page |
|---|---|---|---|---|---|---|---|---|
| 1362 | LBSCR | Five plank Open for carrying propeller cases | Not stated | Not stated | 5071-5120 (second use of numbers) | 50 | Converted from D1369 and renumbered in 1941 | 14 |
| 1363 | LBSCR | Five plank Open Goods (with square ends) | 10 | 5-12 | In D1370 range | At least 31 | Ex-D1370 with round ends removed | 14, 16 |
| 1364 | LBSCR | Five plank Open Goods (with square ends) | 8 & 10 | 5-12 | In D1366 & 1369 ranges | At least 282 | Ex-D1366/69 with round ends removed | 14, 18-22 |
| 1365 (i) | LBSCR | Four plank Open Goods | 6 | 5-2 | 19261-64/73-81 (most numbers were allocated twice during 1923-25, some to three and five plank open goods wagons) | At least 20 | Ex-duplicate stock Few actually renumbered | 11-13 |
| 1365 (ii) | LBSCR | Five plank Open Goods (with square ends) | 10 | 5-9 | In D1368 range | At least 3 | Ex-D1368 with round ends removed Some later to D1364 | 14, 22 |
| 1366 | LBSCR | Five plank Open Goods (with round ends) | 8 | 5-16 | 19282-20681. Also some for loco. coal traffic in 64XXX series | 1400 | Some later to D1364 Some uprated to 10 tons | 14, 17 |
| 1367 | LBSCR | Five plank Open Goods (with square ends) 9ft. 6in. wheelbase | 8 | 5-11 | 20682-21791. Also some for loco. coal traffic in 64XXX series | 1100 | A few numbers were allocated twice to ex-duplicate stock | 14 |
| 1368 | LBSCR | Five plank Open Goods (with round ends and steel underframe) | 10 | 5-16 | 21792-22291 | 500 | Built by contractors Some later to D1365 | 14, 22 |
| 1369 | LBSCR | Five plank Open Goods (with round ends) 9ft. 3in. wheelbase | 10 | 5-16 | 18729-19078, between 22293 and 25273 and 25275-26185, 27462-27711 inc. Also some for loco. coal traffic in 64XXX range and Nos. 27719-27881, 28253-28300/21-28485 on Isle of Wight from 1924 onwards. | At least 3498 | Some built by SR. A few numbers were allocated twice to ex-duplicate stock. Some IOW transfers were not renumbered. Some later to D1362 and 1364 Numbers mixed with D1370 | 14, 19-22 |
| 1370 | LBSCR | Five plank Open Goods (with round ends) 9ft. 6in. wheelbase | 10 | 5-16 | Between 22292 and 25274 (most were between 23666 and 25274). Also some for loco. coal traffic in 64XXX series | At least 1076 | A few numbers were allocated twice to ex-duplicate stock. Some later to D1363 | 14, 16 |
| 1371 | LBSCR | Five plank Open Goods (with round ends and steel underframe) 9ft. 6in. wheelbase | 10 | 6-0 | 26186-27085. Also some for loco. coal traffic in 64XXX series. Some numbers between 26186 and 26208 were actually allocated twice | 900 | Built by contractors Some later to D1375 | 14 |
| 1372 | LBSCR | Six plank Open Goods/Mineral (steel underframe) | 10 | 6-1 | 27086-27236. Also some for loco. coal traffic in 64XXX series | 151 | Built by contractors Some later to D1374 | 24 |
| 1373 | LBSCR | Seven plank Mineral (RCH type) | 12 | 6-17 | 27237-27461 | 225 | Built by contractors to SECR drawings | 25 |
| 1374 (i) | LBSCR | Six plank Open Goods (steel underframe) | 8 | 6-1 | 27146/60/79, 27217 and wagons renumbered into the 64XXX series | At least 18 | Downrated from D1372 about 1926 onwards | 24 |
| 1374 (ii) | LBSCR | Seven plank Open Goods/Mineral | 10 | Not stated | 18780 (mainland), 27545 (Isle of Wight) | 2 | Rebuilt from D1369 | 14, 21 |
| 1375 | LBSCR | Five plank Open Goods (steel underframe) | 8 | 6-0 | 26250/94, 26341, 26557/62/75, 26655/87, 26926/50, 27013/59/66 and wagons renumbered into the 64XXX series | At least 50 | Downrated from D1371, about 1926 onwards | 14 |
| — | LBSCR | Five plank Open Goods | 10 | Not stated | 27719/20 | 2 | Ex-duplicate stock. No details in SR register | 14 |
| — | IWR | Open Goods | 5 | — | 27787 | 1 | | 74 |
| — | IWR | Open Goods (many different designs) | 6 | — | 27788-27821 | 34 | Number 27804 later 8 tons Nos. 27795/97 renumbered as ballast wagons 62903/4, 3/27 | 74-76 |
| — | IWR | Open Goods | 9 | — | 27822-27885 | 64 | Several different designs | 74-76 |
| — | IWR | Open Goods (several different designs) | 10 | — | 27886-27950 | 65 | Some later renumbered as loco. coal wagons Nos. 64348-51 | 74-76 |
| — | IWR | Open Goods | 12 | — | 27951-27971 | 21 | Some later renumbered as loco. coal wagons Nos. 64393-64400 | 74-76 |
| — | IWR | Open Goods | 15 | — | 27972-27975 | 4 | | 74-76 |
| — | IWCR | Open Goods | 6 | — | 27976-27981 | 6 | | 82 |
| — | IWCR | Open Goods (several different designs) | 8 | — | 27982-28131 | 150 | | 78, 82-84 |
| — | IWCR | Open Goods (several different designs) | 10 | — | 28132-28226 | 95 | | 82-84 |
| — | FYNR | Open Goods (see notes) | 8 | — | 28227-28246 | 20 | Includes five rebuilt from cattle wagons by SR, 1923 | 89 |
| — | FYNR | Open Goods | 10 | — | 28247-28252 | 6 | | 89 |
| — | PDSWJR | Three plank Dropside Goods | 8 | 4-13 | None in capital stock | 30 | Survivors to Departmental use at Eastleigh Works | 95 |
| — | PDSWJR | Five plank Open Goods | 8 | 5-2 | None in capital stock | 20 | | 94 |
| 1391 | L&BR | Four plank Bogie Open Goods | 8 | 5-5 | 28313 | 1 | | 100 |
| 1392 | L&BR | Three plank Bogie Open Goods | 6 | 3-18 | 28312 | 1 | | 98 |
| 1393 | L&BR | Four plank Bogie Open Goods | 8 | 5-5 | 28301-28302 | 2 | | 98 |
| 1394 | L&BR | Four plank Open Goods | 4 | 2-16 | 28304-28311 | 8 | | 97 |
| 1395 | L&BR | Four plank Bogie Open Goods | 8 | 6-0 | 28303 | 1 | | 98, 102 |
| 1396 | L&BR | Five plank Bogie Open Goods | 8 | 6-1 | 28316-28319 | 4 | Ordered by SR, 1927 | 102 |
| 1397 | L&BR | Bogie Platform Wagon | 8 | 4-0 | 28314-28315 | 2 | | 100 |

| SR Diagram | Origin | Vehicle Type | Capacity (tons) | Average Tare | SR Running Numbers | Total | Notes | Page |
|---|---|---|---|---|---|---|---|---|
| — | LBSCR | Covered Goods | 7 | Not stated | 46191 (not carried) | 1 | Rebuilt from D1564 goods brake van | 26, 38 |
| 1433 | LBSCR | Covered Goods | 8 | 6-13 | 46192-46620. Also Nos. 46941-48 on Isle of Wight from 1927 onwards. Vans 46311/70/81/89 were for poultry traffic and were Westinghouse-braked | 429 | Some IOW numbers later transposed with D1434 and 1436. Several body variants | 26-28 |
| 1434 | LBSCR | Covered Goods (steel underframe) | 8 | 7-18 | 46621-46718. Also Nos. 46927-39 on Isle of Wight from 1927 onwards | 98 | Built by contractors | 26, 30 |
| 1435 | LBSCR | Covered Goods for egg traffic | 8 | 7-2 | 46719-38 | 20 | | 26, 32 |
| 1436 | LBSCR | Covered Goods | 10 | 6-13 | 46739-73. Also Nos. 46940/49-74 on Isle of Wight from 1927 onwards | 35 | Some Isle of Wight numbers later transposed with D1433/34 | 26, 29 |
| 1457 | LBSCR | Covered Goods (Isle of Wight) | 10 | Not stated | 46924-26 | 3 | Rebuilt in 1935 from D1528 cattle wagons | 26, 36 |
| — | IWR | Covered Goods (several different designs) | 6 | — | 46975-46986 | 12 | Westinghouse brakes | 76-77 |
| — | IWCR | Covered Goods (several different designs) | 8 | — | 46987-47002 | 15 | Westinghouse pipes | 84-85 |
| — | IWCR | Covered Goods (several different designs) | 10 | — | 47003-47031 | 29 | Westinghouse pipes | 84-85 |
| — | FYNR | Covered Goods | 8 | — | 47032-47035 | 4 | No. 47035 with internal handbrake | 89 |
| — | PDSWJR | Covered Goods | 8 | — | None allocated | 2 | | 94 |
| 1453 | L&BR | Covered Goods | 4 | 2-11 | 47036-47041 | 6 | | 97 |
| 1456 | L&BR | Bogie Covered Goods | 8 | 6-6 | 47042-47045 | 4 | Ordered by SR, 1927 | 102 |
| 1471 | LBSCR | Refrigerator Van (Westinghouse-braked) | 9 | 8-16 | 50594/95 | 2 | Scrapped before renumbered | 26, 32 |
| 1527 | LBSCR | Large Cattle Wagon | 6 | 6-13 | 52882-53281 | 400 | Thirty five wagons were Westinghouse-braked. Some later 10 tons | 34 |
| 1528 | LBSCR | Large Cattle Wagon | 10 | 7-3 | 53282-53301. Also Nos. 53371-76 on Isle of Wight from 1927 onwards | 20 | Nos. 53374-76 rebuilt to D1457 in 1935 | 34 |
| 1059 | LBSCR | Special Cattle Wagon | 8 | 7-12 | 3820-31 (Passenger stock series) | 12 | | 36 |
| 1060 | LBSCR | Special Cattle Wagon | 8 | 7-12 | 3832-42 (Passenger stock series) | 11 | | 36 |
| 1061 | LBSCR | Special Cattle Wagon | 9 | Not stated | 3843-48 (Passenger stock series) | 6 | With drover's compartment Similar to horse-boxes | 36 |
| — | IWR | Cattle Wagon | 6 | — | 53377-53379 | 3 | Westinghouse brakes | 77 |
| — | IWCR | Cattle Wagon | 8 | — | 53380-53382 | 3 | Westinghouse brakes | 85 |
| — | IWCR | Cattle Wagon | 10 | — | 53383-53387 | 5 | Westinghouse brakes | 85 |
| 1564 | LBSCR | Goods Brake Van (Stroudley) | 7 | 7-5 | 55586-55608/10-49/51-55722 | 135 | Few renumbered. Nos. 55649/79 may have later been to D1570 | 38-40 |
| 1565 | LBSCR | Goods Brake Van (Stroudley) | 7 | 7-4 | 55723/24 | 2 | Scrapped before re-numbered. As D1564 but with higher roof profile | 38 |
| 1566 | LBSCR | Goods Brake Van (Billinton) | 9 | 9-0 | 55725-31 | 7 | | 38, 40 |
| 1567 | LBSCR | Goods Brake Van (Stroudley) | 9 | 9-10 | 55732-52 | 21 | Few renumbered. Similar to D1564 but 1¾in. narrower | 38 |
| 1568 | LBSCR | Goods Brake Van (Billinton) | 10 | 10-0 | 55753-55841 | 89 | Vans as D1566 | 38, 40 |
| 1569 | LBSCR | Goods Brake Van (Stroudley) | 10 | 10-0 | 55843 (not carried, instead to service stock as 385s) | 1 | Van as D1567 | 38 |
| 1570 | LBSCR | Twin Goods Brake Van (Stroudley) | 7 each | 13-13 overall | 55609 + 55650. Possibly also Nos. 55649 + 55679 in 1924 | 1 pair | Each van as D1564 Paired by Southern Railway | 38 |
| 1571 | LBSCR | Twin Goods Brake Van (Stroudley) | 10 each | 21-10 overall | 55842 + 55848, 55844 + 55847, 55845 + 55846 | 3 pairs | Each van as D1569 Paired by Southern Railway | 38 |
| 1572 | LBSCR | Goods Brake Van (Billinton) | 12 | 12-9 | 55849-62 | 14 | Vans as D1566. No. 55849 later downrated to 10 tons | 38, 40 |
| 1573 | LBSCR | Shunting Truck/Incline Brake | 15 | 14-17 | 55863 (not carried, later allocated the number 61361, not carried either) | 1 | For use at Brighton Lower Yard | 38 |
| 1574 | LBSCR | Goods Brake Van (Panter) | 15 | 15-6 | 55864-77 | 14 | Some later fitted with vacuum pipes | 38, 43 |
| 1575 | LBSCR | Six-wheeled Goods Brake Van (Billinton) | 20 | 20-0 | 55878-96 | 19 | Built by contractors | 38, 42 |
| 1576 | LBSCR | Goods Brake Van (Panter) | 20 | 20-7 | 55897-55927 | 31 | Some built by SR. Many later rebuilt as ballast brake vans, to D1760 | 38, 46 |
| 1577 | LBSCR | Six-wheeled Goods Brake Van (Panter) | 20 | 20-0 | 55928-42 | 15 | | 38, 45 |
| — | IWR | Goods Brake Van | — | — | 56033 | 1 | | 77 |
| — | IWR | Goods Brake Van | 9 | — | 56034 | 1 | To departmental No. 472s in 8/32 | 78 |
| — | IWCR | Goods Brake Van | 7 | 6-16 | 56035/36 | 2 | 56036 to 445s in 9/29 | 87 |
| 1588 | IWCR | Goods Brake Van | 10 | 10-12 | 56037 | 1 | Rebuilt in 1930 | 86-87 |
| — | FYNR | Goods Brake Van | — | — | 56038 | 1 | Stroudley LBSCR vehicle | 90 |
| — | PDSWJR | Goods Brake Van | 10 | 10-19 | 56042/43 | 2 | | 95 |
| 1589 | L&BR | Bogie Goods Brake Van | 8 | 6-0 | 56041 | 1 | | 101 |
| 1590 | L&BR | Bogie Goods Brake Van | 8 | 5-18 | 56039/40 | 2 | | 100 |
| 1616 | LBSCR | Single Bolster 12ft. 0in. long | 6 | 3-18 | 58277-58468. Also Nos. 59037-45/47-52 on Isle of Wight from 1928 onwards | 192 | Many later uprated to 10 tons (Diagram 1619) | 49 |
| 1617 | LBSCR | Single Bolster 13ft. 0in. long | 6 | 4-15 | 58469-58653. Also Nos. 59033-36/46 on Isle of Wight from 1928 onwards | 185 | Many later uprated to 10 tons (Diagram 1620) | 49 |
| 1618 | LBSCR | Double Bolster | 8 | 6-2 | 58654-58784. (wagon No. 58668 had a single bolster only) | 131 | Many later uprated to 10 tons (Diagram 1621) | 49, 51 |
| 1619 | LBSCR | Single Bolster 12ft. 0in. long | 10 | 3-18 | 58785 | 1 | Many more later uprated from Diagram 1616 | 49 |
| 1620 | LBSCR | Single Bolster 13ft. 0in. long | 10 | 4-15 | 58786-58831 | 46 | Many more later uprated from Diagram 1617 | 49 |
| 1621 | LBSCR | Double Bolster (some coupled in pairs) | 10 | 6-2 | 58832-58910. Also Nos. 61066-69 in Engineer's stock from 1930 | 79 | Many more later uprated from Diagram 1618 | 49, 51 |
| — | IWR | Flat Truck | 6 | — | 59011/12/15/16/20 | 5 | Several different designs | 78-79 |
| — | IWR | Timber Truck | 6 | — | 59013/14/17-19 | 5 | Several different designs | 78-79 |
| — | IWR | Flat Truck | 9 | — | 59021-23 | 3 | No. 59021 to 568s in 1931 | 78-79 |
| — | IWCR | Flat Truck | 4 | — | 59024-26 | 3 | | 86 |
| — | IWCR | Timber Truck | 6 | — | 59027 | 1 | | 86 |
| — | IWCR | Timber Truck | 10 | — | 59028-32 | 5 | Several different designs | 86 |

| SR Diagram | Origin | Vehicle Type | Capacity (tons) | Average Tare | SR Running Numbers | Total | Notes | Page |
|---|---|---|---|---|---|---|---|---|
| 1661 | LBSCR | Road Vehicle Truck | 10 | 5-12 | 60423-60545. Also Nos. 60565-83 on Isle of Wight from 1928 onwards | 123 | Some built by SR | 53 |
| 1684 | LBSCR | Plate Glass Wagon | 6 | 6-18 | 61070/71 | 2 | | 53, 59 |
| 1685 | LBSCR | Bogie Aeroplane Truck 38ft. 0in. long | 12 | 11-13 | 61072 | 1 | Underframe ex-bogie refrigerator van in 1923 | 53, 57 |
| 1686 | LBSCR | Machinery Wagon | 20 | 7-1 | 61073-78 | 6 | Coded WELL 'D'. 20ft. 2in. long | 53, 55 |
| 1687 | LBSCR | Bogie Aeroplane Truck 48ft. 0in. long | 20 | 13-2 | 61079-81 | 3 | Ex-bogie timber wagons in 1915 | 53, 57 |
| 1688 | LBSCR | Eight-wheeled Machinery Wagon | 30 | 18-8 | 61082 (later Departmental No. 01159s) | 1 | Boiler trolley | 53, 56 |
| 1689 | LBSCR | Aeroplane Truck 29ft. 11in. long | 4 | 6-12 | 61083/84 | 2 | Reclassified from Diagram 1752 in 7/23 | 53, 58 |
| 1689 | LBSCR | Aeroplane Truck 29ft. 11in. long | 4 | Not stated | 61085 | 1 | Rebuilt from Diagram 1756 in 8/25 | 53, 58 |
| 1705 | LBSCR | Gunpowder Van | 7 | 9-19 | 61261-64 | 4 | | 53, 59 |
| 1713 | IWR | Tar Tank | 15 | — | 61381/82 | 2 | Re-underframed in 1929 | 80 |
| — | IWCR | Tar (later Water) Tank | 10 | — | 61383 | 1 | To 443s, 6/28. | 88 |
| 1716 | Reb. SR | Tar Tank | 17 | 18-4 | 61384/5 | 2 | Re-underframed 1932 Ex-LSWR Tenders 1947 | 92 |
| 1751 | LBSCR | Two plank Ballast Dropside | 4 | 3-13 | 62532-62606. Also Nos. 62905-22 on Isle of Wight from 1927 onwards | 75 | With dumb buffers | 60 |
| 1752 | LBSCR | Points and Crossings Wagon 29ft. 11in. long | 4 | 6-12 | 62607/8 (not carried) | 2 | Reclassified as Diagram 1689 in 7/23 | 60 |
| 1753 | LBSCR | Three plank Ballast Dropside | 6 | 4-1 | 62609-79 | 71 | With dumb buffers | 60 |
| 1754 | LBSCR | Three plank Ballast Dropside | 15 | 6-15 | 62680-62791 | 112 | | 60, 62 |
| 1755 | LBSCR | All-steel Ballast Hopper | 20 | 9-7 | 62792-62821. Ten to Isle of Wight circa 1947, not renumbered | 30 | Built by contractors. Hoppers modified during SR ownership | 60, 63 |
| 1756 | LBSCR | Six-wheeled three plank Ballast Dropside | 20 | Not stated | 62822 (probably not carried) | 1 | Rebuilt as aeroplane truck to Diagram 1689 in 8/25 | 60 |
| 1757 | LBSCR | Ballast Brake Van (Stroudley) | 8 | 7-5 | 62823-25 | 3 | Vans as D1564 | 38-40 |
| 1758 | LBSCR | Ballast Brake Van | 8 | 7-15 | 62826-33 | 8 | Billinton design | 60, 64 |
| 1759 | LBSCR | Six-wheeled Ballast Brake Van | 20 | 20-0 | 62834-39 | 6 | Panter design | 60, 65 |
| 1760 | LBSCR | Ballast Brake Van | 20 | 20-0 | 62840-56 | 17 | Rebuilt from D1576, 1928-37 | 38, 48 |
| — | IWCR | Ballast Wagon | 6 | — | 62881 | 1 | | 88 |
| — | IWCR | Ballast Wagon | 8 | — | 62882/83 | 2 | No. 62883 later 'rebuilt' to Diagram 1352 | 88 |
| — | IWCR | Ballast Wagon | 10 | — | 62884 | 1 | | 88 |
| — | IWR | Ballast Wagon | 6 | — | 62903/4 | 2 | Ex-opens 27795/97 | 75 |
| 1352 | PO/SECR | Four plank Ballast Dropside | 10 | 5-1 | 62885-62904 | 20 | To IOW from 1924 onwards | 90-91 |
| 1798 | LBSCR | Sleeper Wagon | 10 | 5-4 | 64642-47 | 6 | | 67, 70 |
| 1799 | LBSCR | Ballast, Rail and Sleeper Wagon | 12 | 6-19 | 64648-96 | 49 | Built by contractors | 67 |
| 1800 | LBSCR | Rail and Sleeper Wagon | 10 | 6-14 | 64697-64705 | 9 | No. 64704 later 12 tons | 67, 71 |
| 1801 | LBSCR | Rail and Sleeper Wagon | 12 | 6-19 | 64706-25 | 20 | Built by contractors | 67, 71 |
| 1802 | LBSCR | Bogie Rail Wagon | 20 | 19-8 | 64726-37 | 12 | Built by contractors Six later to Diagram 1803 | 67-69 |
| 1803 | LBSCR | Bogie Rail Wagon for carrying long welded rails | 21 | 19-8 | 64728/31/32/33/36/37 | 6 | Converted from D1802 in 1952. Vacuum-piped | 67, 70 |
| — | LBSCR | Points and Crossings Wagon | 12 | 7-9 | 352s-357s (Departmental stock) | 6 | | 67 |

Notes:
1. Some diagram and running numbers were later reallocated to SR-built or converted vehicles.
2. In many cases, identical vehicles existed in Service Department use at the Grouping. Apart from a few examples included in the above list, such service stock has been omitted. Ex-LBSCR vehicles were allocated the following service stock numbers after the Grouping.

Main series 291s-357s (series later reached 1999s)
Duplicate series 0901s-01119s (series later reached 01290s)

Both series were considerably extended during SR ownership, whilst a similar 'DS' prefixed system has been perpetuated since 1948.
Crane match trucks took the same number as the crane, with the suffix 'SM'. Since 1948, these were reallocated new numbers in the 'DS' series and no longer took the same number as their crane.
3. Owing to the diversity of the Isle of Wight wagon types it has not been possible to list every design separately, therefore each group has been broken down by origin and capacity only.
4. After nationalisation, Nos. 21631-6 were reused for second-hand stock inherited from the East Kent Railway.

# Appendix 2
# Standard LBSCR Wagon Dimensions, 1908

## Details taken from a contract specification

| | 8 & 10 Ton Open Wagon | 10 Ton Machinery Wagon | 15 Ton Ballast Wagon | Covered Goods Wagon | Cattle Wagon | Timber Wagon | Goods Brake Van |
|---|---|---|---|---|---|---|---|
| Drawing Number | 5862 | 6238 | 5814 | 6179 | 6153 | 6196 | 4174 |
| Length over buffers | 18ft. 5in. | 19ft. 6in. | 23ft. 0in. | 21ft. 4in. | 21ft. 4in. | 15ft. 0in. | 19ft. 0in. |
| Length over headstocks | 15ft. 5in. | 16ft. 6in. | 20ft. 0in. | 18ft. 4in. | 18ft. 4in. | 12ft. 0in. | 16ft. 1½in. |
| Length over body outside | 15ft. 5in. | 16ft. 6in. | 20ft. 0in. | 18ft. 4in. | 18ft. 4in. | 12ft. 0in. | 16ft. 0in. |
| Length over body inside | 15ft. 0in. | 16ft. 1½in. | 19ft. 7in. | 18ft. 0in. | 18ft. 0in. | 11ft. 7in. | 15ft. 3in. |
| Width over headstocks | 7ft. 9in. | 8ft. 2in. | 8ft. 0in. | 7ft. 10in. | 8ft. 0in. | 7ft. 5in. | 7ft. 10½in. |
| Width over body outside | 7ft. 9in. | 8ft. 2in. | 8ft. 0in. | 7ft. 8½in. | 8ft. 0in. | 7ft. 5in. | 7ft. 9in. |
| Width over body inside | 7ft. 4in. | 7ft. 8in. | 7ft. 7in. | 7ft. 4½in. | 7ft. 5½in. | 6ft. 9½in. | 7ft. 1in. |
| Width over solebars | 6ft. 8½in. | 6ft. 9in. | 6ft. 11in. | 6ft. 8½in. | 6ft. 8½in. | 6ft. 9½in. | 6ft. 9½in. |
| Width inside solebars | 5ft. 11½in. | 5ft. 11½in. | 6ft. 1in. | 5ft. 11½in. | 5ft. 11½in. | 5ft. 11½in. | 5ft. 11½in. |
| Wheelbase | 9ft. 3in. | 10ft. 5in. | 12ft. 0in. | 9ft. 9in. | 11ft. 2in. | 7ft. 0in. | 9ft. 9in. |
| Thickness of flitch plates | — | ¼in. | ½in. | — | — | ½in. | ½in. |
| Headstocks | 12in. x 4½in. | 13¾in. x 4½in. | 12in. x 5in. | 12in. x 4½in. | 12in. x 4½in. | 12in. x 4½in. | See Drawing |
| Solebars and cross members | 12in. x 4½in. | 12in. x 4½in. | 12in. x 4½in. | 12in. x 4½in. | 12in. x 4½in. | 12in. x 4½in. | 12in. x 4½in. |
| Longitudinal timbers (middle) | 12in. x 3in. | 12in. x 3in. | 12in. x 3in. | 12in. x 3in. | 12in. x 3in. | 12in. x 4½in. | 8in. x 4in. |
| Longitudinal timbers (ends) | 12in. x 3in. | 12in. x 3in. | 12in. x 3in. | 12in. x 3in. | 12in. x 3in. | 12in. x 2½in. | 12in. x 4½in. |
| Diagonal timbers | 12in. x 3in. | 12in. x 3in. | 12in. x 3in. | 12in. x 3in. | 12in. x 3in. | 10in. x 3in. | 12in. x 3in. |

Materials to be as follows:

Generally frames were to be of English Oak, Odesa oak, North American white oak or Blackbutt of three years natural seasoning. Frames for brake vans were to be of English or Odesa oak only. Body sheeting was Russian deal, except for the sides of cattle wagons which were to be of pitch pine. Painting — generally inside and out lead colour. Roofs white. Number plates black, lettering and figures white. All ironwork to be black.